The authentic taste of Spain

tapas

The authentic taste of Spain

tapas

Susanna Tee
Linda Doeser

BARNES
& NOBLE
NEW YORK

Cover and Internal Design by Talking Design.
Introduction by Linda Doeser.

2006 Barnes & Noble Publishing

ISBN - 13: 978-0-7607-8481-5
ISBN - 10: 0-7607-8481-7

Printed and bound in China

1 3 5 7 9 10 8 6 4 2

Notes for reader
This book uses imperial, metric or US cup measurements. Follow the same units of
measurements throughout, do not mix imperial and metric. All spoon measurements
are level: teaspoons are assumed to be 5ml, and tablespoons are assumed to be 15ml.
Unless otherwise stated, milk is assumed to be low fat and eggs are medium. The times
given are an approximate guide only.

Some recipes contain nuts. If you are allergic to nuts you should avoid using them and
any products containing nuts. Recipes using raw or very lightly cooked eggs should be
avoided by infants, the elderly, pregnant women, convalescents and anyone suffering
from illness.

contents

INTRODUCTION

Nowadays there are tapas bars in cities across the world, yet not long ago hardly anyone outside Spain knew what tapas were. These delicious cocktail snacks range from tiny stuffed tomatoes to spicy shrimp kabobs, from fat squares of warm tortilla to elegant seafood tartlets, and from simple cubes of serrano ham to fried baby eels served so hot that they burn your mouth.

Tapas have come a long way from their beginnings—in style as well as geographically. Spain has a hot and dry climate, so working hours and mealtimes were organized to make the most of the cooler parts of the day. Dinner was rarely eaten before late evening, so it became customary to drop in to a bar on the way home from work for a glass of sherry, wine, or hard cider. Bars in Andalucía, the region of southern Spain where sherry is produced, took to covering their customers' glasses with a slice of bread to keep flies out of the drinks. The word tapa means lid or cover. Later, they began to add a topping of ham or cheese, providing a complimentary snack.

From Andalucía, the custom of serving bar snacks spread across Spain, eventually giving rise to specialty tapas bars. Here customers order from an extensive menu and pay for these tasty little mouthfuls. The city of Barcelona in northern Spain is now arguably the tapas capital of the country.

Serving and eating tapas

Tapas have now become a course in their own right, rather like Italian antipasti and Greek *"meze"*. A selection of dishes is often served as an hors d'oeuvre before the main course of a conventional meal. However, they have become so popular that people have taken to dining solely on tapas, choosing a larger selection to include a more extensive range of ingredients. Nevertheless, tapas haven't completely lost their historical beginnings and are still served as cocktail snacks in private houses.

Of course, home cooks can choose to serve tapas however they like. A table of tapas dishes is a popular choice for informal entertaining, as it tends to be colorful, fun, and full of all sorts of different tastes and textures. Everyone is sure to find a favorite. Tapas dishes make great appetizers on more formal occasions and are a fuss-free way to overcome the difficulty of entertaining both vegetarian and meat-eating guests. Returning them to their roots, you may choose to serve them as tempting snacks with pre-dinner drinks and they also look fabulous on a buffet table at a party.

Some tapas are still served on the traditional base of bread or toast which is often rubbed with garlic for extra flavor. Those with simple toppings, such as ham, cheese, mushrooms, or shrimp, are usually assembled in the kitchen and may be garnished with an herb sprig or twist of lemon. Toppings that more closely resemble a dip or pâté in texture are often served in a bowl with the toast handed separately for guests to help themselves. This prevents the toast from becoming soggy. The tapas that come next in the evolutionary chain are those served in pastry shells, on mini-pizza bases, or in little turnovers called empanadillas. Remember that all of these snacks should be bite-size, so cut or stamp out the bases and shells accordingly.

Increasingly, tapas dishes have developed away from the idea of a bread or pastry base, although most are still finger

foods. These include olives, almonds, mussels served on the half shell, stuffed baby vegetables and eggs, and miniature kabobs. Some, such as deep-fried shrimp and boiled new potatoes, are served with a dip. Finally, there are tapas that resemble small entrees—meat, chicken, fish, or vegetables cooked in sauce. Again, these should all be individual bite-size morsels.

In Spain, tapas are almost always served in earthenware dishes. Hot foods can be cooked in them and cold snacks stay cool, but you don't have to go out and buy a whole new set of serving dishes. Use small dishes that suit the size of the serving. Dishes that are too big will make the contents look skimpy and inadequate and if you're serving a selection of tapas, you'll probably run out of room on the table.

Provide a good supply of wooden toothpicks for spearing olives, shrimp, and so on. This helps limit the rather unhygienic practice of lots of different hands rummaging around in the serving dishes. If you're serving tapas as an appetizer or as an informal meal, you should also supply plates, knives, and forks.

The authentic flavor of Spain

All the recipes in the following pages are based on both traditional and contemporary Spanish cooking and eating habits. Many of the ingredients will be familiar, even to those who have never visited the Mediterranean. Wherever a typically Spanish ingredient that may be difficult to obtain is specified an alternative is suggested in the recipe or in the glossary of ingredients below.

ANCHOVY: Fresh anchovies are easily spoiled so they are rarely available in inland cities in Spain, let alone in non-Mediterranean countries. Whole, salted anchovies, however, are widely used in tapas recipes and are well worth using if you can find them. As they are not always available in supermarkets elsewhere, the recipes in this book suggest using canned anchovy fillets. Both types can be soaked in milk or water to remove some of the salt, and whole anchovies should be filleted before use.

CHORIZO: This spicy, red sausage is also widely used in Mexican cooking. There are many varieties, some much hotter than others, but all contain pork and paprika, the spice producing the characteristic color. It is important to distinguish between chorizo produced for slicing and eating and chorizo intended for cooking.

CLAMS: Small European varieties, such as carpetshell, are the most popular for tapas dishes. Cherrystones or littlenecks are an equivalent size.

MANCHEGO: Made from sheep's milk, Manchego is Spain's best-known cheese. Originally produced in La Mancha, it is now made throughout the country and widely exported. It has a nutty flavor and is pale in color. It is sold at all ages from young fresco Manchego to sharp cheese known as Iberico. Depending on the recipe, Parmesan or Swiss cheese may be substituted.

OLIVE OIL: Spain is probably the world's largest producer of olive oil. It is characteristically deep gold in color and tends to be lighter and less pungent than Italian and Greek varieties of olive oils.

OLIVES: Both green and black olives feature in many tapas dishes and a bowl of olives is a cocktail snack in its own right. Andalucía is the largest area of production and Gordal and Manzanilla olives are the best-known varieties. Green olives are frequently stuffed with pimientos, almonds, or onion. In the Basque region, green olives stuffed with anchovies are a specialty.

PAPRIKA: This dark red spice is made from ground red bell peppers. It may be mild, sometimes called sweet, or hot but is never so fiery as cayenne. In Spanish paprika production the bell peppers are smoked first, giving the spice a very distinctive flavor. Smoked paprika is available from some specialty stores.

PIMIENTOS: These are simply sweet bell peppers, but to non-Spaniards pimientos usually implies a variety of long, thin bell pepper that has been cooked, peeled, and preserved in oil. They may be sliced or whole.

SAFFRON: Pungent with a slightly bitter taste, saffron is the world's most expensive spice. The neighboring regions of La Mancha and Valencia are said to produce the best saffron in the world. There is no substitute.

SERRANO HAM: Jamón serrano simply means mountain ham and refers to ham that is salted for about a week and air-dried for six months. It is eaten raw, like prosciutto, which may be used as a substitute. Spanish ham is quite chewy in texture as it is carved with rather than against the grain.

SHERRY: This drink, which gets it name from Jerez de la Frontera, the blisteringly hot, dry, chalky region of Andalucía where it is produced, is a fortified wine. Of course, tapas were developed to go with sherry in the first place, but, in turn, sherry is often used to flavor tapas dishes. Other regions of Spain make a similar wine, notably Montilla from Montilla-Moriles and a sweet wine from Málaga.

VINEGAR: Both regular red and white wine vinegar are used in salad dressings and cooking, but Spain also produces specialty wine vinegars. Rioja vinegar, usually red, is full-bodied like the wine and mellow in flavor. Sherry vinegar is dark, mellow, rounded, and smooth. Both are available from some specialty stores and sherry vinegar, in particular, is worth searching for if you want a truly authentic Spanish flavor to your food. Balsamic vinegar may be used as a substitute.

Salads & Savory Bites

A SALAD OF MELON, CHORIZO & ARTICHOKES

SERVES 8
as part of a tapas meal

12 small globe artichokes

juice of 1/2 lemon

2 tbsp Spanish olive oil

1 small orange-fleshed melon, such as cantaloupe

7 oz/200 g chorizo sausage, outer casing removed

a few sprigs of fresh tarragon or flat-leaf parsley, to garnish

DRESSING

3 tbsp Spanish extra virgin olive oil

1 tbsp red wine vinegar

1 tsp prepared mustard

1 tbsp chopped fresh tarragon

salt and pepper

To prepare the artichokes, cut off the stalks. With your hands, break off the toughest outer leaves at the base until the tender inside leaves are visible. Using a pair of scissors, cut the spiky tips off the leaves. Using a sharp knife, pare the dark green skin from the base and down the stem. As you prepare them, brush the cut surfaces of the artichokes with lemon juice to prevent discoloration. Alternatively, you could fill a bowl with cold water to which you have added a little lemon juice, and immerse the artichokes in the acidulated water to stop discoloration. Carefully remove the choke (the mass of silky hairs) by pulling it out with your fingers or by scooping it out with a spoon. It is very important to remove all the choke as the little barbs, if eaten, can irritate the throat. However, if you are using very young artichokes, you do not need to worry about removing the choke and you can include the stalk too, well scraped, as it will be quite tender. Cut the artichokes into quarters and brush them again with lemon juice.

Heat the olive oil in a large, heavy-bottom skillet, then add the prepared artichokes and cook, stirring frequently, for 5 minutes, or until the artichoke leaves are golden brown. Remove from the skillet, transfer to a large serving bowl, and let cool.

To prepare the melon, cut in half and scoop out the seeds with a spoon. Cut the flesh into bite-size cubes. Add to the cooled artichokes. Cut the chorizo into bite-size chunks and add to the melon and artichokes.

To make the dressing, put all the ingredients in a small bowl and whisk together. Just before serving, pour the dressing over the prepared salad ingredients and toss together. Serve the salad garnished with tarragon or parsley sprigs.

OLIVES WRAPPED WITH ANCHOVIES

Using a sharp knife, halve each anchovy fillet lengthwise.

Wrap a half fillet around the middle of each olive, overlapping the ends, and secure with a wooden toothpick.

Repeat with another olive and anchovy fillet half and slide onto the toothpick.

Continue until all the ingredients are used. Serve immediately or cover until required.

MAKES 12

12 anchovy fillets in oil, drained

24 pimiento- or almond-stuffed olives, drained

SWEET ONION SALAD

Bring a large pan of lightly salted water to a boil. Add the onions and simmer for 20 minutes, or until tender. Drain and let stand until cool enough to handle.

Thickly slice the onions and place in a shallow dish. Sprinkle over the parsley and olives and season to taste with pepper.

Whisk the vinegars and olive oil together in a bowl, then whisk in enough of the water to make a creamy vinaigrette.

Pour the dressing over the onions and serve at room temperature.

**SERVES 4–6
as part of a tapas
meal**

4 Spanish or bermuda
onion

2 tbsp chopped fresh
parsley

$^2/_3$ cup black olives,
pitted

1 tbsp sherry vinegar

2 tbsp red wine vinegar

$^1/_2$ cup Spanish olive oil

about 1 tbsp water

salt and pepper

CRACKED MARINATED OLIVES

To allow the flavors of the marinade to penetrate the olives, place on a cutting board and, using a rolling pin, bash them lightly so that they crack slightly. Alternatively, use a sharp knife to cut a lengthwise slit in each olive as far as the pit. Using the flat side of a broad knife, lightly crush each garlic clove. Using a mortar and pestle, crack the coriander seeds. Cut the lemon, with its rind, into small chunks.

Put the olives, garlic, coriander seeds, lemon chunks, thyme sprigs, fennel, and chiles, if using, in a large bowl and toss together. Season with pepper to taste, but you should not need to add salt as preserved olives are usually salty enough. Pack the ingredients tightly into a glass jar with a lid. Pour in enough olive oil to cover the olives, then seal the jar tightly.

Let the olives stand at room temperature for 24 hours, then marinate in the refrigerator for at least 1 week but preferably 2 weeks before serving. From time to time, gently give the jar a shake to remix the ingredients. Return the olives to room temperature and remove from the oil to serve. Provide toothpicks for spearing the olives.

SERVES 8
as part of a tapas meal

1 lb/450 g can or jar unpitted large green olives, drained

4 garlic cloves, peeled

2 tsp coriander seeds

1 small lemon

4 sprigs of fresh thyme

4 feathery stalks of fennel

2 small fresh red chiles (optional)

pepper

Spanish extra virgin olive oil, to cover

SAUTÉED GARLIC MUSHROOMS

SERVES 6
as part of a tapas meal

1 lb/450 g white mushrooms

5 tbsp Spanish olive oil

2 garlic cloves, finely chopped

squeeze of lemon juice

salt and pepper

4 tbsp chopped fresh flat-leaf parsley

crusty bread, to serve

Wipe or brush clean the mushrooms, then trim off the stalks close to the caps. Cut any large mushrooms in half or into quarters. Heat the olive oil in a large, heavy-bottom skillet, add the garlic and cook for 30 seconds–1 minute, or until lightly browned. Add the mushrooms and sauté over high heat, stirring most of the time, until the mushrooms have absorbed all the oil in the skillet.

Reduce the heat to low. When the juices have come out of the mushrooms, increase the heat again, and sauté for 4–5 minutes, stirring most of the time, until the juices have almost evaporated. Add a squeeze of lemon juice and season to taste with salt and pepper. Stir in the parsley and cook for an additional minute.

Transfer the sautéed mushrooms to a warmed serving dish and serve piping hot or warm. Accompany with chunks or slices of crusty bread for mopping up the garlic cooking juices.

RUSSIAN SALAD

Put the eggs in a pan, cover with cold water, and slowly bring to a boil. Immediately reduce the heat to very low, cover and let simmer gently for 10 minutes. As soon as the eggs are cooked, drain them and put under cold running water. By doing this quickly, you will prevent a black ring from forming round the egg yolk. Gently tap the eggs to crack the egg shells and leave them until cold.

Meanwhile, put the potatoes in a large pan of cold, salted water and bring to a boil. Lower the heat and let simmer for 7 minutes, or until just tender. Add the beans and peas to the pan for the last 2 minutes of cooking. Drain well, splash under cold running water, then let the vegetables cool completely.

Cut the carrots into julienne strips about 1 inch/2.5 cm in length. Flake the tuna into large chunks. When the potatoes, beans, and peas are cold, put them in a large bowl. Add the carrot strips and the flaked tuna and very gently toss the ingredients together. Transfer the vegetables and tuna to a salad bowl or large serving dish.

In a pitcher, stir the lemon juice into the mayonnaise to thin it slightly, then stir in the garlic and season to taste with salt and pepper. Drizzle the mayonnaise dressing over the vegetables and tuna.

Sprinkle the gherkins, olives, and capers into the salad and finally sprinkle over the parsley and dill. You can store the salad in the refrigerator but return to room temperature before serving. Just before serving, crack the shells of the eggs all over and remove them. Slice the eggs into wedges, add them to the salad, and garnish with dill sprigs.

SERVES 8
as part of a tapas meal

2 eggs

1 lb/450 g baby new potatoes, quartered

4 oz/115 g green beans, cut into 1-inch/ 2.5-cm lengths

1 cup frozen peas

4 oz/115 g carrots

7 oz/200 g canned tuna steak in olive oil, drained

2 tbsp lemon juice

1/2 cup mayonnaise

1 garlic clove, crushed

salt and pepper

4 small gherkins, sliced

8 pitted black olives, halved

1 tbsp capers

1 tbsp chopped fresh flat-leaf parsley

1 tbsp chopped fresh dill, plus extra sprigs to garnish

SALTED ALMONDS

**SERVES 6–8
as part of a tapas
meal**

scant 1¹/₂ cups whole
almonds, in their skins
or blanched
(see directions)

4 tbsp Spanish olive oil

coarse sea salt

1 tsp paprika or ground
cumin (optional)

Preheat the oven to 350°F/180°C. Fresh almonds in their skins are superior in taste, but blanched almonds are much more convenient. If the almonds are not blanched, put them in a bowl, cover with boiling water for 3–4 minutes, then plunge them into cold water for 1 minute. Drain them well in a strainer, then slide off the skins between your fingers. Dry the almonds well on paper towels.

Put the olive oil in a roasting pan and swirl it round so that it covers the bottom. Add the almonds and toss them in the pan so that they are evenly coated in the oil, then spread them out in a single layer.

Roast the almonds in the oven for 20 minutes, or until they are light golden brown, tossing several times during the cooking. Drain the almonds on paper towels, then transfer them to a bowl.

While the almonds are still warm, sprinkle with plenty of sea salt and the paprika or cumin, if using, and toss well together to coat. Serve the almonds warm or cold. The almonds are at their best when served freshly cooked, so, if possible, cook them on the day that you plan to eat them. However, they can be stored in an airtight container for up to 3 days.

TOMATO & OLIVE SALAD

First, make the dressing. Whisk the vinegar, olive oil, garlic, and paprika together in a bowl. Season to taste with salt and reserve.

Place the tomatoes, olives, cucumber, shallots, and capers in a separate bowl. Pour over the dressing and toss lightly.

Line 6 individual serving bowls with chicory leaves. Spoon an equal quantity of the salad into the center of each and serve.

**SERVES 6
as part of a tapas
meal**

2 tbsp sherry or red
wine vinegar

5 tbsp Spanish olive oil

1 garlic clove, finely
chopped

1 tsp paprika

4 tomatoes, peeled and
diced

12 anchovy-stuffed or
pimiento-stuffed olives

$^1/_2$ cucumber, peeled
and diced

2 shallots, finely
chopped

1 tbsp pickled capers
in brine, drained

2–3 heads of chicory,
separated into leaves

salt

TUNA, EGG & POTATO SALAD

**SERVES 4
as part of a tapas
meal**

12 oz/350 g new
potatoes, unpeeled

1 hard-cooked egg,
cooled
and shelled

3 tbsp Spanish olive oil

1¹/₂ tbsp white wine
vinegar

4 oz/115 g canned
tuna in oil, drained and
flaked

2 shallots, finely
chopped

1 tomato, peeled and
diced

2 tbsp chopped fresh
parsley

salt and pepper

Cook the potatoes in a pan of lightly salted boiling water for 10 minutes, then remove from the heat, cover, and let stand for 15–20 minutes, or until tender.

Meanwhile, slice the egg, then cut each slice in half. Whisk the olive oil and vinegar together in a bowl and season to taste with salt and pepper. Spoon a little of the vinaigrette into a serving dish to coat the base.

Drain the potatoes, then peel and thinly slice. Place half the slices over the base of the dish and season to taste with salt, then top with half the tuna, half the egg slices, and half the shallots. Pour over half the remaining dressing. Make a second layer with the remaining potato slices, tuna, egg, and shallots, then pour over the remaining dressing.

Finally, top the salad with the tomato and parsley. Cover with plastic wrap and let stand in a cool place for 1–2 hours before serving.

CHORIZO IN RED WINE

Before you start, bear in mind that this dish is best if prepared the day before you are planning to serve it.

Using a fork, prick the chorizo sausage in 3 or 4 places. Put it in a large pan and pour in the wine. Bring the wine to a boil, then lower the heat, cover, and let simmer gently for 15–20 minutes. Transfer the chorizo and wine to a bowl or dish, cover, and let the sausage marinate in the wine for 8 hours or overnight.

The next day, remove the chorizo from the bowl or dish and reserve the wine for later. Remove the outer casing from the chorizo and cut the sausage into ¼-inch/5-mm slices.

Place the slices in a large, heavy-bottom skillet or ovenproof serving dish.

If you are adding the brandy, pour it into a small pan and heat gently. Pour the brandy over the chorizo slices, stand well back, and set alight. When the flames have died down, shake the pan gently, add the reserved wine to the pan, and cook over high heat until almost all of the wine has evaporated.

Serve the chorizo in red wine piping hot, in the dish in which it was cooked, sprinkled with parsley to garnish. Accompany with chunks or slices of bread to mop up the juices and provide toothpicks with which to spear the chorizo.

**SERVES 6
as part of a tapas
meal**

7 oz/200 g chorizo
sausage

scant 1 cup Spanish
red wine

2 tbsp brandy
(optional)

chopped fresh flat-leaf
parsley, to garnish

crusty bread, to serve

TUNA ROLLS

Preheat the broiler to high. Place the bell peppers on a baking sheet and cook under the preheated broiler, turning frequently, for 10 minutes, until the skin is blackened and blistered all over. Using tongs, transfer to a plastic bag, then tie the top and let cool.

Meanwhile, whisk the olive oil, lemon juice, vinegar, garlic, paprika, chile flakes, and sugar together in a small bowl.

When the peppers are cool enough to handle, peel off the skins, then cut the flesh into quarters lengthwise and seed. Place the pepper pieces in a nonmetallic dish and pour over the dressing, turning to coat. Let stand in a cool place for 30 minutes.

Rub the salt off the capers and mix with the tuna. Drain the pepper pieces, reserving the dressing. Divide the tuna mixture among the pepper pieces and roll up. Secure with a wooden toothpick. Place the tuna rolls on a serving platter, then spoon over the dressing and serve at room temperature.

**SERVES 4
as part of a tapas
meal**

3 red bell peppers

1/2 cup Spanish olive oil

2 tbsp lemon juice

5 tbsp red wine vinegar

2 garlic cloves, finely
chopped

1 tsp paprika

1 tsp dried chile flakes

2 tsp sugar

2 tbsp salted capers

7 oz/200 g canned
tuna in oil, drained and
flaked

GREEN BEANS WITH PINE NUTS

Heat the oil in a large, heavy-bottom skillet, add the pine nuts and cook for about 1 minute, stirring all the time and shaking the skillet, until light golden brown. Using a slotted spoon, remove the pine nuts from the skillet, drain well on paper towels, then transfer to a bowl. Set aside the oil in the skillet for later. Add the paprika, according to taste, to the pine nuts, stir together until coated, and then set aside.

Trim the green beans and remove any strings if necessary. Put the beans in a pan, pour over boiling water, return to a boil, and cook for 5 minutes, or until tender but still firm. Drain well in a strainer.

Reheat the oil in the skillet, add the onion and cook for 5–10 minutes, or until softened and starting to brown. Add the garlic and cook for an additional 30 seconds.

Add the beans to the skillet and cook for 2–3 minutes, tossing together with the onion until heated through. Season the beans to taste with salt and pepper.

Turn the contents of the skillet into a warmed serving dish, sprinkle over the lemon juice, and toss together. Sprinkle over the golden pine nuts and serve hot.

SERVES 8
as part of a tapas meal

2 tbsp Spanish olive oil

scant 1/3 cup pine nuts

1/2–1 tsp paprika

1 lb/450 g green beans

1 small onion, finely chopped

1 garlic clove, finely chopped

salt and pepper

juice of 1/2 lemon

STUFFED PIMIENTOS

**MAKES 7–8
as part of a tapas
meal**

6¹/₂ oz/185 g canned
or bottled whole
pimientos del piquillo
(fire-roasted sweet red
peppers)

fresh herb sprigs,
to garnish

**CURD CHEESE AND
HERB FILLING**

1 cup curd cheese

1 tsp lemon juice

1 garlic clove, crushed

4 tbsp chopped fresh
flat-leaf parsley

1 tbsp chopped fresh
mint

1 tbsp chopped fresh
oregano

salt and pepper

OR

**TUNA MAYONNAISE
FILLING**

7 oz/200 g canned
tuna steak in olive oil,
drained

5 tbsp mayonnaise

2 tsp lemon juice

2 tbsp chopped fresh
flat-leaf parsley

salt and pepper

OR

**GOAT CHEESE AND
OLIVE FILLING**

scant ¹/₃ cup pitted
black olives,
finely chopped

7 oz/200 g soft goat
cheese

1 garlic clove, crushed

salt and pepper

There is a choice of fillings provided in this recipe—the final decision is yours.

Lift the peppers from the jar, reserving the oil for later.

To make the Curd Cheese and Herb Filling, put the curd cheese in a bowl and add the lemon juice, garlic, parsley, mint, and oregano. Mix well together. Season to taste with salt and pepper.

To make the Tuna and Mayonnaise Filling, put the tuna in a bowl and add the mayonnaise, lemon juice, and parsley. Add 1 tablespoon of the reserved oil from the jar of pimientos and mix well. Season to taste with salt and pepper.

To make the Goat Cheese and Olive Filling, put the olives in a bowl, and add the goat cheese, garlic, and 1 tablespoon of the reserved oil from the jar of pimientos. Mix well together. Season to taste with salt and pepper.

Using a teaspoon, heap the filling of your choice into each pimiento. Put in the refrigerator and let chill for at least 2 hours until firm.

To serve the pimientos, arrange them on a serving plate and, if necessary, wipe with paper towels to remove any of the filling that has spread over the skins. Garnish with herb sprigs.

ARTICHOKE HEARTS & ASPARAGUS

Trim and discard the coarse, woody ends of the asparagus spears. Make sure all the stems are about the same length, then tie them together loosely with clean kitchen string. If you have an asparagus steamer, you don't need to tie the stems together—just place them in the basket.

Bring a tall pan of lightly salted water to a boil. Add the asparagus, making sure that the tips are protruding above the water, then reduce the heat and let simmer for 10–15 minutes, or until tender. Test by piercing a stem just above the water level with the point of a sharp knife. Drain, then refresh under cold running water and drain again.

Cut the asparagus spears into 1-inch/2.5-cm pieces, keeping the tips intact. Cut the artichoke hearts into small wedges and combine with the asparagus in a bowl.

Whisk the orange juice, orange rind, walnut oil, and mustard together in a bowl and season to taste with salt and pepper. If serving immediately, pour the dressing over the artichoke hearts and asparagus and toss lightly.

Arrange the salad greens in individual serving dishes and top with the artichoke and asparagus mixture. Serve immediately. Alternatively, store the salad, covered, in the refrigerator and add the dressing just before serving.

**SERVES 4
as part of a tapas
meal**

1 lb/450 g asparagus
spears

14 oz/400 g canned
artichoke hearts,
drained and rinsed

2 tbsp freshly
squeezed orange juice

1/2 tsp finely grated
orange rind

2 tbsp walnut oil

1 tsp Dijon mustard

salt and pepper

salad greens, to serve

MIXED BEANS

Bring a large pan of lightly salted water to a boil. Add the fava beans and reduce the heat, then cover and simmer for 7 minutes. Remove the beans with a slotted spoon, then plunge into cold water and drain. Remove and discard the outer skins.

Meanwhile, return the pan of salted water to a boil. Add the green beans and return to a boil again. Drain and refresh under cold running water. Drain well.

Mix the fava beans, green beans, snow peas, and shallot together in a bowl. Strip the leaves from the mint sprigs, then reserve half and add the remainder to the bean mixture. Finely chop the reserved mint.

Whisk the olive oil, vinegar, garlic, and chopped mint together in a separate bowl and season to taste with salt and pepper. Pour the dressing over the bean mixture and toss lightly to coat. Cover with plastic wrap and let chill until required.

**SEVES 4–6
as part of a tapas
meal**

6 oz/175 g shelled
fresh or frozen fava
beans

4 oz/115 g fresh or
frozen green beans

4 oz/115 g snow peas,
trimmed

1 shallot, finely
chopped

6 fresh mint sprigs

4 tbsp Spanish olive oil

1 tbsp sherry vinegar

1 garlic clove, finely
chopped

salt and pepper

 ROASTED BELL PEPPER SALAD

Preheat the broiler. Place the bell peppers on a wire rack or broiler pan and cook under a hot broiler for 10 minutes, until their skins have blackened and blistered, turning them frequently.

Remove the broiled bell peppers from the heat, put them in a bowl, and immediately cover tightly with a clean, damp dish towel. Alternatively, you can put the bell peppers in a plastic bag. You will find that the steam helps to soften the skins and makes it easier to remove them. Let the peppers stand for about 15 minutes, until they are cool enough to handle.

Holding one bell pepper at a time over a clean bowl, use a sharp knife to make a small hole in the base and gently squeeze out the juices and reserve them. Still holding the bell pepper over the bowl, carefully peel off the blackened skin with your fingers or a knife and discard it. Cut the bell peppers in half and remove the stem, core, and seeds, then cut each bell pepper into neat thin strips. Arrange the bell pepper strips attractively on a serving dish.

To the reserved pepper juices add the olive oil, sherry vinegar, garlic, sugar, and salt and pepper to taste. Whisk together until combined. Drizzle the dressing evenly over the salad.

Sprinkle the capers, olives, and chopped marjoram over the salad, garnish with marjoram sprigs, and serve at room temperature.

SERVES 8
as part of a tapas meal

3 red bell peppers

3 yellow bell peppers

5 tbsp Spanish extra virgin olive oil

2 tbsp dry sherry vinegar or lemon juice

2 garlic cloves, crushed

pinch of sugar

salt and pepper

1 tbsp capers

8 small black Spanish olives

2 tbsp chopped fresh marjoram, plus extra sprigs to garnish

STUFFED BELL PEPPERS

MAKES 6

6 tbsp Spanish olive oil, plus a little extra for rubbing on bell peppers

2 onions, finely chopped

2 garlic cloves, crushed

2/3 cup Spanish short-grain rice

1/3 cup raisins

1/3 cup pine nuts

generous 1/2 cup fresh parsley, finely chopped

1 tbsp tomato paste dissolved in 3 cups hot water

salt and pepper

6 red, green, or yellow bell peppers (or a mix of colors)

Preheat the oven to 400°F/200°C. Heat the oil in a shallow, heavy-bottom flameproof casserole. Add the onions and cook for 3 minutes. Add the garlic and cook for an additional 2 minutes, or until the onion is soft but not brown.

Stir in the rice, raisins, and pine nuts until all are coated in the oil, then add half the parsley and salt and pepper to taste. Stir in the tomato paste and bring to a boil. Reduce the heat and let simmer, uncovered, shaking the casserole frequently, for 20 minutes, or until the rice is tender, the liquid is absorbed and small holes appear on the surface. Watch carefully because the raisins can catch and burn. Stir in the remaining parsley, then let cool slightly.

While the rice is simmering, cut the top off each bell pepper and reserve. Remove the core and seeds from each bell pepper.

Divide the stuffing equally between the bell peppers. Use wooden toothpicks to secure the tops back in place. Lightly rub each bell pepper with olive oil and arrange in a single layer in a baking dish. Bake in the preheated oven for 30 minutes, or until the bell peppers are tender. Serve hot or let cool to room temperature.

Egg & Cheese Dishes

STUFFED CHERRY TOMATOES

**SERVES 8
as part of a tapas
meal**

24 cherry tomatoes

**ANCHOVY AND OLIVE
FILLING**

1³/₄ oz/50 g canned
anchovies in olive oil

8 pimiento-stuffed
green olives, finely
chopped

2 large hard-cooked
eggs, finely chopped

pepper

OR

CRAB SALAD FILLING

6 oz/175 g canned
crabmeat, drained

4 tbsp mayonnaise

1 tbsp chopped fresh
flat-leaf parsley

salt and pepper

OR

**BLACK OLIVE AND
CAPER FILLING**

12 pitted black olives

3 tbsp capers

6 tbsp Aïoli
(see page 164)

salt and pepper

Several different choices of filling have been given in this recipe, so make a decision before you start, or, of course, you could make a selection of each. Simply cut the filling quantities to stuff the corresponding number of tomatoes.

If necessary, cut and discard a very thin slice from the stalk end of each tomato to make the bases flat and stable. Cut a thin slice from the smooth end of each tomato and discard. Using a serrated knife or teaspoon, loosen the pulp and seeds of each and scoop out, discarding the flesh. Turn the scooped-out tomatoes upside down on paper towels and let drain for 5 minutes.

To make the Anchovy and Olive Filling, drain the anchovies, reserving the oil for later, chop finely, and put in a bowl. Add the olives and hard-cooked eggs. Pour in a trickle of oil from the drained anchovies to moisten the mixture, season with pepper (don't add salt to season as the anchovies will provide enough) and mix well together.

To make the Crab Salad Filling, put the crabmeat, mayonnaise, and parsley in a bowl and mix well together. Season the filling to taste with salt and pepper.

To make the Black Olive and Caper Filling, put the olives and capers on paper towels to drain them well, then chop finely and put in a bowl. Add the Aïoli and mix well together. Season the filling to taste with salt and pepper.

Fill a pastry bag fitted with a ³/₄-inch/2-cm plain tip with the filling of your choice and use to pack the filling into the hollow tomato shells. Store the tomatoes in the refrigerator until ready to serve.

DEEP-FRIED MANCHEGO CHEESE

Slice the cheese into triangular shapes about ³/₄ inch/2 cm thick or alternatively into cubes measuring about the same size. Put the flour in a plastic bag and season with salt and pepper to taste. Break the egg into a shallow dish and beat together with the water. Spread the bread crumbs onto a plate.

Toss the cheese pieces in the flour so that they are evenly coated, then dip the cheese in the egg mixture. Finally, dip the cheese in the bread crumbs so that the pieces are coated on all sides. Transfer to a large plate and store in the refrigerator until you are ready to serve them.

Just before serving, heat about 1 inch/2.5 cm of the corn oil in a large, heavy-bottom skillet or heat the oil in a deep-fryer to 350–375°F/ 180–190°C, or until a cube of bread browns in 30 seconds. Add the cheese, in batches of about 4 or 5 pieces so that the temperature of the oil does not drop, and deep-fry for 1–2 minutes, turning once, until the cheese is just starting to melt and the pieces are golden brown on all sides. Do make sure that the oil is hot enough, otherwise the coating on the cheese will take too long to become crisp and the cheese inside may ooze out.

Using a slotted spoon, remove the deep-fried cheese from the skillet or deep-fryer and drain well on paper towels. Serve the deep-fried cheese pieces hot, accompanied by toothpicks on which to spear them.

SERVES 6–8
as part of a tapas
meal

7 oz/200 g manchego
cheese

3 tbsp all-purpose flour

salt and pepper

1 egg

1 tsp water

1¹/₂ cups fresh white
or brown bread crumbs

corn oil, for deep-frying

DEVILED EGGS

MAKES 16

8 large eggs

2 whole pimientos
(sweet red peppers)
from a jar or can

8 pitted green olives,
retain the slices
for garnishing

5 tbsp mayonnaise

8 drops Tabasco sauce

large pinch of cayenne
pepper

salt and pepper

paprika, for dusting

sprigs of fresh dill, to
garnish

To cook the eggs, put them in a pan, cover with cold water, and slowly bring to a boil. Immediately reduce the heat to very low, cover, and let simmer gently for 10 minutes. As soon as the eggs are cooked, drain, and put under cold running water. By doing this quickly, it will prevent a black ring from forming round the egg yolk. Gently tap the eggs to crack the egg shells and let them stand until cold. When cold, crack the shells all over and remove them.

Using a stainless steel knife, halve the eggs lengthwise, then carefully remove the yolks. Put the yolks in a nylon strainer, set over a bowl, and rub through, then mash them with a wooden spoon or fork. If necessary, rinse the egg whites under cold water and dry very carefully.

Put the pimientos on paper towels to dry well, then chop them finely, reserving a few strips. Finely chop the olives. If you are going to pipe the filling into the eggs, you need to chop both these ingredients very finely so that they will go through a 1/2-inch/1-cm tip. Add the chopped pimientos and most of the chopped olives to the mashed egg yolks, reserving 16 larger pieces to garnish. Add the mayonnaise, mix well together, then add the Tabasco sauce, cayenne pepper, and salt and pepper to taste.

For a grand finale, put the egg yolk mixture into a pastry bag fitted with a 1/2-inch/1-cm plain tip and pipe the mixture into the hollow egg whites. Alternatively, for a simpler finish, use a teaspoon to spoon the prepared filling into each egg half.

Arrange the eggs on a serving plate. Add a small strip of the reserved pimientos and a piece of olive to the top of each stuffed egg. Dust with a little paprika and garnish with dill sprigs.

CHORIZO & CHEESE TORTILLA

Cook the potatoes in a small pan of lightly salted boiling water for 15–20 minutes, or until just tender. Drain and let stand until cool enough to handle, then dice.

Heat the olive oil in a large skillet that can safely be placed under the broiler. Add the onion, bell pepper, and tomatoes and cook over low heat, stirring occasionally, for 5 minutes. Add the diced potatoes and chorizo and cook for an additional 5 minutes. Meanwhile, preheat the broiler to high.

Beat the eggs with the water and salt and pepper to taste in a large bowl. Pour the mixture into the skillet and cook for 8–10 minutes, or until the underside is set. Lift the edge of the tortilla occasionally to let the uncooked egg run underneath. Sprinkle the grated cheese over the tortilla and place under the hot broiler for 3 minutes, or until the top is set and the cheese has melted. Serve, warm or cold, cut into thin wedges.

SERVES 8
as part of a tapas meal

2 small potatoes (peeled)

4 tbsp olive oil

1 small onion, chopped

1 red bell pepper, seeded and chopped

2 tomatoes, seeded and diced

5 oz/140 g chorizo sausage, finely chopped

8 large eggs

2 tbsp cold water

2 oz/55 g sharp Mahon, Manchego, or Parmesan cheese, grated

salt and pepper

BAKED TOMATO NESTS

MAKES 4

4 large ripe tomatoes

4 large eggs

4 tbsp heavy cream

4 tbsp grated sharp
Mahon, Manchego, or
Parmesan cheese

salt and pepper

Preheat the oven to 350°F/180°C. Cut a slice off the top of each tomato and, using a teaspoon, carefully scoop out the pulp and seeds without piercing the shells. Turn the tomato shells upside down on paper towels and let drain for 15 minutes. Season the insides of the shells with salt and pepper.

Place the tomatoes in an ovenproof dish just large enough to hold them in a single layer. Carefully break 1 egg into each tomato shell, then top with 1 tablespoon of cream and 1 tablespoon of grated cheese.

Bake in the preheated oven for 15–20 minutes, or until the eggs are just set. Serve hot.

FAVA BEANS WITH CHEESE & SHRIMP

Bring a large pan of lightly salted water to a boil. Add the fava beans and 1 thyme sprig, then reduce the heat and simmer, covered, for 7 minutes. Drain well and refresh under cold running water, then drain again.

Unless the fava beans are very young, remove and discard the outer skins. Place the beans in a bowl and add the shrimp and cheese.

Chop the remaining thyme sprig. Whisk the olive oil, lemon juice, garlic, and chopped thyme together in a separate bowl and season to taste with salt and pepper.

Pour the dressing over the bean mixture. Toss lightly and serve.

**SERVES 6
as part of a tapas
meal**

1 lb 2 oz/500 g shelled
fresh or frozen fava
beans

2 fresh thyme sprigs

8 oz/225 g cooked
shelled shrimp

8 oz/225 g Queso
Majorero or Gruyère
cheese, diced

6 tbsp Spanish olive oil

2 tbsp lemon juice

1 garlic clove, finely
chopped

salt and pepper

ASPARAGUS & FRIED EGGS

**SERVES 6
as part of a tapas
meal**

1 lb 2 oz/500 g
asparagus spears

2 tbsp Spanish olive oil

6 eggs

Trim and discard the coarse, woody ends of the asparagus spears. Make sure all the stems are about the same length, then tie them together loosely with clean kitchen string. If you have an asparagus steamer, you don't need to tie the stems together—just place them in the basket.

Bring a tall pan of lightly salted water to a boil. Add the asparagus, making sure that the tips are protruding above the water, then reduce the heat and let simmer for 10–15 minutes, or until tender. Test by piercing a stem just above the water level with the point of a sharp knife.

Meanwhile, heat a little of the olive oil in a large, heavy-bottom skillet. Add 2 eggs, if there is enough room, and cook over medium-low heat, or until the whites are just set and the yolks are still runny. Transfer to warmed serving plates and cook the remaining eggs in the same way.

Drain the asparagus and divide the spears among the plates. Serve immediately.

ROASTED BELL PEPPERS WITH FIERY CHEESE

Preheat the broiler to high. Place the bell peppers, skin-side up, in a single layer on a baking sheet. Cook under the hot broiler for 8–10 minutes, or until the skins have blistered and blackened. Using tongs, transfer to a plastic bag. Tie the top and let cool.

When the bell peppers are cool enough to handle, peel off the skin with your fingers or a knife and discard it. Place on a serving plate and sprinkle over the cheese.

Whisk the honey and vinegar together in a bowl and season to taste with salt and pepper. Pour the dressing over the bell peppers, then cover and let chill until required.

SERVES 6
as part of a tapas meal

1 red bell pepper, halved and seeded

1 orange bell pepper, halved and seeded

1 yellow bell pepper, halved and seeded

4 oz/115 g Afuega'l Pitu cheese or other hot spiced cheese, diced

1 tbsp clear honey

1 tbsp sherry vinegar

salt and pepper

MEDITERRANEAN SCRAMBLED EGGS

**SERVES 4–6
as part of a tapas
meal**

3–4 tbsp Spanish
olive oil

1 large onion, finely
chopped

1 large red bell pepper,
seeded and chopped

1 large green bell
pepper, seeded
and chopped

2 large tomatoes,
peeled, seeded, and
chopped

2 oz/55 g chorizo
sausage, sliced thinly,
outer casing removed,
if preferred

generous 2 tablespoons
butter

10 large eggs, lightly
beaten

salt and pepper

4–6 thick slices
country-style bread,
toasted, to serve

Heat 2 tablespoons of olive oil in a large, heavy-bottom skillet over medium heat. Add the onion and bell peppers and cook for 5 minutes, or until the vegetables are softened but not browned. Add the tomatoes and heat through. Transfer to a heatproof plate and keep warm in a preheated low oven.

Add another tablespoon of oil to the skillet. Add the chorizo and cook for 30 seconds, just to warm through and flavor the oil. Add the sausage to the reserved vegetables.

Add a little extra olive oil, if necessary, to bring it back to 2 tablespoons. Add the butter and let melt. Season the eggs with salt and pepper, then add to the pan and scramble until cooked to the desired degree of firmness. Return the vegetables to the pan and stir through. Serve immediately with hot toast.

HARD-COOKED EGGS WITH BELL PEPPERS

Bring a pan of water to a boil. Add the bell peppers and blanch for 5 minutes. Drain, then refresh under cold running water and drain well again. Pat dry with paper towels and cut into thin strips.

Arrange the slices of egg on plates and sprinkle over the bell pepper strips.

Alternatively, make a lattice pattern with the bell pepper strips.

Whisk the vinegar, olive oil, shallot, dill, and sugar together in a bowl and season to taste with salt and pepper. Spoon the dressing over the eggs and serve immediately.

**SERVES 6
as part of a tapas
meal**

2 red bell peppers,
halved and seeded

6 hard-cooked eggs,
cooled, shelled, and
sliced

2 tbsp white wine
vinegar

5 tbsp Spanish olive oil

1 shallot, finely chopped

2 tsp chopped fresh dill

pinch of sugar

salt and pepper

EGGS & CHEESE

Cut the eggs in half lengthwise and, using a teaspoon, carefully scoop out the yolks into a fine strainer, reserving the egg white halves. Rub the yolks through the strainer into a bowl and add the grated cheese, mayonnaise, chives, chile, and salt and pepper to taste.

Spoon the filling into the egg white halves.

Arrange a bed of lettuce on individual serving plates and top with the eggs. Cover and let chill until ready to serve.

SERVES 6
as part of a tapas
meal

6 hard-cooked eggs,
cooled and shelled

3 tbsp grated Manchego
or Cheddar cheese

1–2 tbsp mayonnaise

2 tbsp snipped fresh
chives

1 fresh red chile, seeded
and finely chopped

salt and pepper

lettuce leaves, to serve

SPINACH & MUSHROOM TORTILLA

Heat the olive oil in a skillet that can safely be placed under the broiler. Add the shallots and cook over low heat, stirring occasionally, for 5 minutes, or until softened. Add the mushrooms and cook, stirring frequently, for an additional 4 minutes. Add the spinach, then increase the heat to medium and cook, stirring frequently, for 3–4 minutes, or until wilted. Reduce the heat, then season to taste with salt and pepper and stir in the slivered almonds.

Beat the eggs with the parsley, water, and salt and pepper to taste in a bowl. Pour the mixture into the skillet and cook for 5–8 minutes, or until the underside is set. Lift the edge of the tortilla occasionally to let the uncooked egg run underneath. Meanwhile, preheat the broiler to high.

Sprinkle the grated cheese over the tortilla and cook under the preheated hot broiler for 3 minutes, or until the top is set and the cheese has melted. Serve, room temperature or cold, cut into thin wedges.

**SERVES 4
as part of a tapas
meal**

2 tbsp Spanish olive oil

3 shallots, finely
chopped

12 oz/350 g
mushrooms, sliced

10 oz/280 g fresh
spinach leaves, coarse
stems removed

2 oz/55 g toasted
slivered almonds

5 eggs

2 tbsp chopped fresh
parsley

2 tbsp cold water

3 oz/85 g sharp Mahon,
Manchego, or Parmesan
cheese, grated

salt and pepper

CHEESE & SHALLOTS WITH HERB DRESSING

**SERVES 6
as part of a tapas
meal**

1 tsp sesame seeds

1/4 tsp cumin seeds

4 tomatoes, seeded
and diced

5 tbsp Spanish olive oil

4 tbsp lemon juice

2 tsp chopped fresh
thyme

1 tbsp chopped fresh
mint

4 shallots, finely
chopped

1 lb 2 oz/500 g Idiazabal
or other sheep's milk
cheese, diced

salt and pepper

Dry-roast the sesame and cumin seeds in a small, heavy-bottom skillet, shaking the skillet frequently, until they begin to pop and give off their aroma. Remove the skillet from the heat and let cool.

Place the tomatoes in a bowl. To make the dressing, whisk the olive oil and lemon juice together in a separate bowl. Season to taste with salt and pepper, then add the thyme, mint, and shallots, and mix well.

Place the cheese in another bowl. Pour half the dressing over the tomatoes and toss lightly. Cover with plastic wrap and let chill for 1 hour. Pour the remaining dressing over the cheese, then cover and chill for 1 hour.

To serve, divide the cheese mixture among 6 serving plates and sprinkle with half the toasted seeds. Top with the tomato mixture and sprinkle with the remaining toasted seeds.

STUFFED EGGS

Cut the eggs in half lengthwise and, using a teaspoon, carefully scoop out the yolks into a fine strainer, reserving the egg white halves. Rub the yolks through the strainer into a bowl.

Mash the sardines with a fork, then mix with the egg yolks. Stir in the lemon juice and Tabasco, then add enough mayonnaise to make a paste. Season to taste with salt and pepper.

Spoon the filling into the egg white halves, mounding it up well. Spread out the flour and bread crumbs in separate shallow dishes. Dip each egg half first in the flour, then in the beaten egg and finally in the bread crumbs.

Heat the vegetable oil for deep-frying in a deep-fat fryer or large pan to 350–375°F/180–190°C, or until a cube of bread browns in 30 seconds. Deep-fry the egg halves, in batches if necessary, for 2 minutes, or until golden brown. Drain on paper towels and serve hot, garnished with parsley sprigs.

**SERVES 6
as part of a tapas
meal**

6 hard-cooked eggs,
cooled and shelled

4$^1/_4$ oz/120 g canned
sardines in olive oil,
drained

4 tbsp lemon juice

dash of Tabasco sauce

1–2 tbsp mayonnaise

$^1/_3$ cup all-purpose flour

1$^1/_2$ cups fresh white
bread crumbs

1 large egg, lightly
beaten

vegetable oil, for deep-
frying

salt and pepper

fresh parsley sprigs, to
garnish

OVEN-BAKED TORTILLA

MAKES 48 PIECES

Spanish olive oil

1 large garlic clove,
crushed

4 scallions, white and
green parts finely
chopped

1 green bell pepper,
seeded and finely diced

1 red bell pepper,
seeded and finely diced

6 oz/175 g potato,
boiled, peeled, and diced

5 large eggs

scant 1/2 cup sour cream

6 oz/175 g freshly
grated Spanish Roncal
cheese, or Cheddar, or
Parmesan cheese

3 tbsp snipped fresh
chives

salt and pepper

green salad, to serve

Preheat the oven to 375°F/190°C. Line a
7 x 10-inch/18 x 25-cm shallow baking pan
with foil and brush with olive oil. Reserve.

Place a little olive oil, the garlic, scallions,
and peppers in a skillet and cook over medium
heat, stirring, for 10 minutes, or until the scallions
are softened but not browned. Let cool, then
stir in the potato.

Beat the eggs, sour cream, cheese, and
chives together in a large bowl. Stir the cooled
vegetables into the egg mixture and season
to taste with salt and pepper.

Pour the mixture into the baking sheet and
smooth over the top. Bake in the preheated

oven for 30–40 minutes, or until golden brown,
puffed and set in the center. Remove from
the oven and let cool and set. Run a spatula
around the edge, then invert onto a baking
sheet, and peel off the foil. If the surface
looks a little runny, place it under a medium
broiler to dry out.

Let cool completely. Trim the edges if
necessary, then cut into 48 squares. Serve
on a platter with wooden toothpicks, or secure
each square to a slice of bread, and accompany
with a green salad.

FLAMENCO EGGS

Preheat the oven to 350°F/180°C. Heat the olive oil in a large, heavy-bottom skillet. Add the onion and garlic and cook over low heat, stirring occasionally, for 5 minutes, or until softened. Add the red bell peppers and cook, stirring occasionally, for an additional 10 minutes. Stir in the tomatoes and parsley, season to taste with salt and cayenne pepper and cook for an additional 5 minutes. Stir in the corn kernels and remove the skillet from the heat.

Divide the mixture among 4 individual ovenproof dishes. Make a hollow in the surface of each using the back of a spoon. Break an egg into each depression.

Bake in the preheated oven for 15–25 minutes, or until the eggs have set. Serve hot.

SERVES 4

4 tbsp Spanish olive oil

1 onion, thinly sliced

2 garlic cloves, finely chopped

2 small red bell peppers, seeded and chopped

4 tomatoes, peeled, seeded, and chopped

1 tbsp chopped fresh parsley

7 oz/200 g canned corn kernels, drained

4 eggs

salt and cayenne pepper

The Baker's Choice

GARLIC PAN-FRIED BREAD & CHORIZO

**SERVES 6–8
as part of a tapas
meal**

7 oz/200 g chorizo
sausage, outer casing
removed

4 thick slices 2-day-old
country bread

Spanish olive oil, for
pan-frying

3 garlic cloves, finely
chopped

2 tbsp chopped fresh
flat-leaf parsley

paprika, to garnish

Cut the chorizo sausage into ½-inch/1-cm thick slices and cut the bread, with its crusts still on, into ½-inch/1-cm cubes. Add enough olive oil to a large, heavy-bottom skillet so that it generously covers the bottom. Heat the oil, add the garlic, and cook for 30 seconds– 1 minute, or until lightly browned.

Add the bread cubes to the skillet and pan-fry, stirring all the time, until golden brown and crisp. Add the chorizo slices and pan-fry for 1–2 minutes, or until hot. Using a slotted spoon, remove the bread cubes and chorizo from the skillet and drain well on paper towels.

Turn the pan-fried bread and chorizo into a warmed serving bowl, add the chopped parsley, and toss together. Garnish the dish with a sprinkling of paprika and serve warm. Accompany with toothpicks so that a piece of sausage and a cube of bread can be speared together for eating.

CHORIZO EMPANADILLAS

Preheat the oven to 400°F/200°C. Cut the chorizo sausage into small dice measuring about ½ inch/1 cm square.

On a lightly floured counter, thinly roll out the puff pastry. Using a plain, round 3¼-inch/8-cm cutter, cut into circles. Gently pile the trimmings together, roll out again, then cut out additional circles to produce 12 in total. Put about a teaspoonful of the chopped chorizo onto each of the pastry circles.

Dampen the edges of the pastry with a little water, then fold one half over the other half to completely cover the chorizo. Seal the edges together with your fingers. Using the prongs of a fork, press against the edges to give a decorative finish and seal them further. With the tip of a sharp knife, make a small slit in the side of each pastry. You can store the pastries in the refrigerator at this stage until you are ready to bake them.

Place the pastries onto dampened baking sheets and brush each with a little beaten egg to glaze. Bake in the oven for 10–15 minutes, or until golden brown and puffed. Using a small strainer, lightly dust the top of each empanadilla with a little paprika to garnish. Serve the chorizo empanadillas hot or warm.

MAKES 12

4¹/₂ oz/125 g chorizo
sausage, outer casing
removed

all-purpose flour, for
dusting

9 oz/250 g prepared
puff pastry, thawed if
frozen

beaten egg, to glaze

paprika, to garnish

CHEESE & HAM PASTRIES

MAKES 6

6 slices serrano ham

Tabasco sauce, for
brushing

7 oz/200 g Queso
Majorero, Manchego, or
goat cheese

6 sheets phyllo dough,
about 18 x 11 inches/
46 x 28 cm

3–4 tbsp Spanish
olive oil

Preheat the oven to 400°F/200°C. Spread out the ham and brush with Tabasco to taste. Cut the cheese into 6 slices. Wrap a slice of cheese in each slice of ham.

Working on one sheet of phyllo dough at a time and keeping the others covered with a clean, damp kitchen towel, brush with a little olive oil, then fold in half. Place 1 ham-wrapped slice of cheese in the center, then brush the phyllo dough with oil again and fold it over to enclose the cheese completely. Place on a baking sheet, seam-side down, and brush the top with a little oil. Repeat with the remaining sheets of phyllo dough and ham-wrapped cheese.

Bake in the preheated oven for 15 minutes, or until golden brown and crisp. Serve immediately or let cool slightly and serve warm.

CRAB TARTLETS

Preheat the oven to 375°F/190°C. To prepare the crabmeat filling, heat the olive oil in a heavy-bottom skillet, add the onion and cook for 5 minutes, or until softened but not browned. Add the garlic and cook for an additional 30 seconds. Add a splash of wine and cook for 1–2 minutes, or until most of the wine has evaporated.

Lightly whisk the eggs in a large mixing bowl, then whisk in the milk or cream. Add the crabmeat, cheese, and parsley, and the onion mixture. Season the mixture with nutmeg, and salt and pepper to taste and mix well together.

To prepare the pie dough if you are making it yourself, mix the flour and salt together in a large mixing bowl. Add the butter, cut into small pieces, and rub in until the mixture resembles fine bread crumbs. Gradually stir in enough of the water to form a firm dough. Alternatively, the pie dough could be made in a food processor.

On a lightly floured counter, thinly roll out the dough. Using a plain, round 2³/₄-inch/7-cm cutter, cut the pastry into 18 circles. Gently pile the trimmings together, roll out again, then cut out an additional 6 circles. Use to line 24 x 1¹/₂-inch/4-cm tartlet pans. Carefully spoon the crabmeat mixture into the pastry shells, taking care not to overfill them.

Bake the tartlets in the oven for 25–30 minutes, or until golden brown and set. Serve the crab tartlets hot or cold, garnished with fresh dill sprigs.

MAKES 24

1 tbsp Spanish olive oil

1 small onion, finely chopped

1 garlic clove, finely chopped

splash of dry white wine

2 eggs

²/₃ cup milk or light cream

6 oz/175 g canned crabmeat, drained

¹/₂ cup Manchego or Parmesan cheese, grated

2 tbsp chopped fresh flat-leaf parsley

pinch of freshly grated nutmeg

salt and pepper

sprigs of fresh dill, to garnish

PIE DOUGH

2¹/₄ cups all-purpose flour, plus extra for dusting

pinch of salt

1¹/₂ sticks/175 g butter

2 tbsp cold water

OR

1 lb 2 oz/500 g prepared unsweetened pastry dough

SPANISH SPINACH & TOMATO PIZZAS

MAKES 32

2 tbsp Spanish olive oil, plus extra for brushing and drizzling

1 onion, finely chopped

1 garlic clove, finely chopped

14 oz/400 g canned chopped tomatoes

scant 3 cups baby spinach leaves

4 tbsp pine nuts

salt and pepper

BREAD DOUGH

4 tbsp warm water

1/2 tsp active dry yeast

pinch of sugar

generous 1 1/4 cups white bread flour, plus extra for dusting

1/2 tsp salt

To make the bread dough, measure the water into a small bowl, sprinkle in the dry yeast and sugar, and let stand in a warm place for 10–15 minutes, or until frothy.

Meanwhile, sift the flour and salt into a large bowl. Make a well in the center of the flour and pour in the yeast liquid, then mix together with a wooden spoon. Using your hands, work the mixture until it leaves the sides of the bowl clean.

Turn the dough out onto a lightly floured counter and knead for 10 minutes, or until smooth and elastic, and no longer sticky. Shape into a ball and put it in a clean bowl. Cover with a clean, damp dish towel and let stand in a warm place for 1 hour, or until the dough has risen and doubled in size.

To make the topping, heat the olive oil in a large, heavy-bottom skillet. Add the onion and cook for 5 minutes, or until softened but not browned. Add the garlic and cook for an additional 30 seconds. Stir in the tomatoes and cook for 5 minutes, letting the mixture bubble and stirring occasionally, until reduced and thickened. Add the spinach leaves and cook, stirring, until they have wilted a little. Season the mixture to taste with salt and pepper.

While the dough is rising, preheat the oven to 400°F/200°C. Brush several baking sheets with olive oil. Turn the dough out onto a lightly floured counter and knead well for 2–3 minutes to knock out the air bubbles. Roll out the dough very, very thinly and, using a 2 1/2-inch/6-cm plain, round cutter, cut out 32 circles. Place on the prepared baking sheets.

Spread each base with the spinach mixture to cover, then sprinkle the pine nuts over the top. Drizzle a little olive oil over each pizza. Bake in the oven for 10–15 minutes, or until the edges of the dough are golden brown. Serve the spinach and tomato pizzas hot.

ANCHOVY ROLLS

Preheat the oven to 425°F/220°C. Lightly grease a baking sheet. Place the anchovies in a small, shallow dish and pour over the milk. Let soak for 10–15 minutes. Drain, discarding the milk, and pat dry with paper towels.

Spread each bread slice with butter and then with mustard. Sprinkle with the grated cheese. Divide the anchovies among the bread slices and roll up.

Place on the baking sheet, seam-side down, and bake in the preheated oven for 6–7 minutes. Let cool slightly, then serve.

MAKES 4

butter, for greasing and spreading

8 salted anchovies, filleted

$^1/_4$ cup milk

4 slices white bread, crusts removed

1 tbsp Dijon mustard

2 tbsp grated Manchego or Cheddar cheese

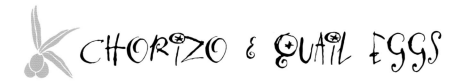

CHORIZO & QUAIL EGGS

Preheat the broiler to high. Arrange the slices of bread on a baking sheet and broil until golden brown on both sides.

Cut or fold the chorizo slices to fit on the toasts, then reserve.

Heat a thin layer of olive oil in a large skillet over medium heat until a cube of bread browns—about 40 seconds. Break the eggs into the skillet and cook, spooning the oil over the yolks, until the whites are set and the yolks are cooked to your liking.

Remove the fried eggs from the skillet and drain on paper towels. Immediately transfer to the chorizo-topped toasts and dust with paprika. Season to taste with salt and pepper, then garnish with parsley and serve immediately.

MAKES 12

12 slices French bread, sliced on the diagonal, about 1/4 inch/5 mm thick

1 1/2 oz/40 g cured, ready-to-eat chorizo, cut into 12 thin slices

Spanish olive oil

12 quail eggs

mild paprika

salt and pepper

fresh flat-leaf parsley, to garnish

CHEESE & OLIVE EMPANADILLAS

Preheat the oven to 400°F/200°C. Cut the cheese into small dice measuring about 1/4 inch/5 mm. Chop the olives, sun-dried tomatoes, and anchovies into pieces about the same size as the cheese. Put all the chopped ingredients in a bowl, season with pepper to taste, and gently mix together. Stir in the sundried tomato paste.

On a lightly floured counter, thinly roll out the puff pastry. Using a plain, round 3¼-inch/8-cm cutter, cut into 18 circles. Gently pile the trimmings together, roll out again, then cut out an additional 8 circles. Using a teaspoon, put a little of the prepared filling equally in the center of each of the pastry circles.

Dampen the edges of the pastry with a little water, then bring up the sides to completely cover the filling and pinch the edges together with your fingers to seal them. With the tip of a sharp knife, make a small slit in the top of each pastry. You can store the pastries in the refrigerator at this stage until you are ready to bake them.

Place the pastries onto dampened baking sheets and brush each with a little beaten egg to glaze. Bake in the oven for 10–15 minutes, or until golden brown, crisp and well risen. Serve the empanadillas piping hot, warm, or cold.

MAKES 26

3 oz/85 g firm or soft cheese

1/2 cup pitted green olives

1/4 cup sun-dried tomatoes in oil, drained

1³/4 oz/50 g canned anchovies, drained

pepper

2 tbsp sun-dried tomato paste

all-purpose flour, for dusting

1 lb 2 oz/500 g prepared puff pastry, thawed if frozen

beaten egg, to glaze

FLATBREAD WITH VEGETABLES & CLAMS

**SERVES 4–6
as part of a tapas
meal**

2 tbsp Spanish extra
virgin olive oil

4 large garlic cloves,
crushed

2 large onions, thinly
sliced

10 pimientos del
piquillo, drained, patted
dry, and thinly sliced

9 oz/250 g shelled
baby clams in brine
(weight in jar), drained
and rinsed

salt and pepper

DOUGH

2²/₃ cups white bread
flour, plus extra for
dusting

1 envelope active dry
yeast

1 tsp salt

¹/₂ tsp sugar

1 tbsp Spanish olive oil,
plus extra for oiling

1 tbsp dry white wine

1 cup warm water

To make the dough, stir the flour, yeast, salt, and sugar together in a bowl, making a well in the center. Add the olive oil and wine to the water, then pour ¹/₄ cup of the liquid into the well. Gradually mix in the flour from the sides, adding the remaining liquid if necessary, until a soft dough forms.

Turn out the dough onto a lightly floured counter and knead until smooth. Shape the dough into a ball. Wash the bowl and rub the inside with olive oil. Return the dough to the bowl and roll it around until lightly coated in oil. Cover the bowl tightly with plastic wrap and let stand in a warm place until the dough doubles in size.

Heat the olive oil in a large, heavy-bottom skillet over medium heat. Reduce the heat and add the garlic and onions and cook slowly, stirring frequently, for 25 minutes, or until the onions are golden brown but not burned.

Preheat the oven to 450°F/230°C. Transfer the onions to a bowl and let cool. Add the sweet pepper strips and clams to the bowl and stir together. Reserve.

Knock back the dough and knead quickly on a lightly floured counter. Cover it with the upturned bowl and let stand for 10 minutes, which will make it easier to roll out.

Heavily flour a 12³/₄ x 12³/₄-inch/ 32 x 32-cm shallow baking sheet. Roll out the dough to make a 13¹/₂-inch/34-cm square and transfer it to the baking sheet, rolling the edges to form a thin rim. Prick the base all over with a fork.

Spread the topping evenly over the dough and season to taste with salt and pepper. Bake in the preheated oven for 25 minutes, or until the rim is golden brown and the onions tips are slightly tinged. Transfer to a wire rack to cool completely. Cut into 12–16 slices.

ONION & OLIVE CIRCLES

Heat the olive oil in a heavy-bottom skillet. Add the onion and garlic and cook over low heat, stirring occasionally, for 15 minutes, or until golden brown and very soft. Stir in the thyme and season to taste with salt and pepper.

Meanwhile, cut off and discard the crusty ends of the bread, then cut the loaf into 8 slices. Toast on both sides, then spread with tapenade or butter.

Pile the onion mixture onto the slices of toast and top each slice with an anchovy fillet and the olives. Serve hot.

**SERVES 4–8
as part of a tapas
meal**

2 tbsp Spanish olive oil

1 onion, thinly sliced

1 garlic clove, finely
chopped

2 tsp chopped fresh
thyme

1 small loaf of French
bread

1 tbsp tapenade or
butter

8 canned anchovy
fillets in
oil, drained

12 olives stuffed with
almonds or onion,
halved

salt and pepper

SHRIMP TOASTS

Halve 1 of the garlic cloves and reserve. Finely chop the remaining cloves. Heat 2 tablespoons of the olive oil in a large, heavy-bottom skillet. Add the chopped garlic and onion and cook over low heat, stirring occasionally, for 5 minutes, or until softened.

Stir in the beans and tomatoes, and season to taste with salt and pepper. Cook gently for an additional 5 minutes.

Meanwhile, toast the bread on both sides, then rub each slice with the cut sides of the reserved garlic and drizzle with the remaining oil.

Stir the shrimp into the bean mixture and heat through gently for 2–3 minutes. Pile the bean and shrimp mixture onto the toasts and serve immediately, garnished with watercress.

SERVES 4

3 garlic cloves

4 tbsp Spanish olive oil

1 Spanish or Bermuda onion, halved and finely chopped

14 oz/400 g canned great Northern beans, drained and rinsed

4 tomatoes, diced

4 thick slices country bread

10 oz/280 g cooked shelled shrimp

salt and pepper

watercress, to garnish

OLIVE & RED BELL PEPPER BREAD

Preheat the broiler to high. Place the bell pepper halves, skin-side up, in a single layer on a baking sheet. Cook under the hot broiler for 8–10 minutes, or until the skin is blackened and blistered all over. Using tongs, transfer to a plastic bag, then tie the top and let cool. When cool enough to handle, peel off the skin.

Finely chop 1 of the garlic cloves. Place in a food processor or blender with the bell pepper halves, capers, parsley, lemon juice, cumin, and sugar and process until smooth.

Scrape the mixture into a bowl and stir in the olives.

Cut off and discard the crusty ends of the bread, then cut the bread into $1/2$-inch/1-cm slices. Toast the slices on both sides. Cut the remaining garlic cloves in half, then rub the cut sides all over the toast. Brush the toast with the olive oil.

Spoon the bell pepper mixture onto the toasted bread and place on a serving platter. Serve immediately.

**SERVES 4–6
as part of a tapas
meal**

2 red bell peppers,
halved and seeded

3 garlic cloves

2 tsp capers, drained,
rinsed, and halved

4 tbsp chopped fresh
parsley

1 tbsp lemon juice

1 tsp ground cumin

2 tsp sugar

$1/3$ cup black olives,
pitted and chopped

1 loaf of French bread

2 tbsp Spanish olive oil

ASPARAGUS ROLLS

MAKES 8

1 stick butter, softened,
plus extra for greasing

8 asparagus spears,
trimmed

8 slices white bread,
crusts removed

1 tbsp chopped fresh
parsley

finely grated rind of 1
orange

salt and pepper

Preheat the oven to 375°F/190°C and lightly grease a baking sheet. If woody, peel the asparagus stems, then tie the spears loosely together with clean kitchen string. Blanch in a tall pan of boiling water for 3–5 minutes. Drain and refresh under cold running water. Drain again and pat dry with paper towels.

Lightly flatten the slices of bread with a rolling pin. Mix a generous ½ stick of the butter, the parsley, and orange rind together in a bowl and season to taste with salt and pepper. Spread the flavored butter over the bread slices.

Place an asparagus spear near one side of a bread slice and roll up. Repeat with the remaining asparagus spears and bread. Place the asparagus rolls, seam-side down, on the baking sheet.

Melt the remaining butter in a small pan, then brush it over the asparagus rolls. Bake in the preheated oven for 15 minutes, or until crisp and golden brown. Let cool slightly, then serve warm.

TOMATO TOASTS WITH THREE TOPPINGS

Toast the bread on both sides. Meanwhile, place the diced tomato in a bowl and mix in the garlic. Spread the tomato mixture evenly over the toast, then season to taste with salt and pepper and drizzle with the olive oil.

For the ham and caper topping, arrange the strips of ham in an "S" shape across 4 of the toasts. Place a caper in the curves of each letter "S."

For the chorizo and cheese topping, place 2 slices of chorizo on each of 4 of the remaining toasts and top with the cheese. Garnish with an olive half.

For the anchovy and olive topping, curl the anchovy fillets into circles. Place 3 circles on each of the remaining 4 toasts and put an olive slice in the center of each.

SERVES 4–6

12 thick slices country bread

12 tomatoes, peeled, seeded, and diced

8 garlic cloves, finely chopped

about 1 1/2 cups Spanish olive oil

salt and pepper

HAM & CAPER TOPPING

2 slices ham, cut into thin strips

8 capers, drained and rinsed

CHORIZO & CHEESE TOPPING

8 slices ready-to-eat chorizo sausage

2 oz/55 g Manchego or Cheddar cheese, sliced

2 pimiento-stuffed olives, halved

ANCHOVY & OLIVE TOPPING

12 canned anchovy fillets in oil, drained

4 anchovy-stuffed green olives, cut widthwise into 3

Fish & Meat Morsels

Sizzling Chile Shrimp

**SERVES 8
as part of a tapas
meal**

1 lb 2 oz/500 g raw
jumbo shrimp, in their
shells

1 small fresh red chile

6 tbsp Spanish olive oil

2 garlic cloves, finely
chopped

pinch of paprika

salt

crusty bread, to serve

To prepare the shrimp, pull off their heads. With your fingers, peel off their shells, leaving the tails intact. Using a sharp knife, make a shallow slit along the back of each shrimp, then pull out the dark vein and discard. Rinse the shrimp under cold water and dry well on paper towels.

Cut the chile in half lengthwise, remove the seeds, and finely chop the flesh. It is important either to wear gloves or to wash your hands very thoroughly after chopping chiles because their juices can cause irritation to sensitive skin, especially around the eyes, nose, or mouth.

Whatever you do, don't rub your eyes after touching the cut flesh of the chile.

Heat the olive oil in a large, heavy-bottom skillet or flameproof casserole until quite hot, then add the garlic and cook for 30 seconds. Add the shrimp, chile, paprika, and a pinch of salt and cook for 2–3 minutes, stirring all the time, until the shrimp turn pink and start to curl.

Serve the shrimp in the cooking dish, still sizzling. Accompany with toothpicks, to spear the shrimp, and chunks or slices of crusty bread to mop up the aromatic cooking oil.

MINIATURE PORK BROCHETTES

The brochettes are marinated overnight, so remember to do this in advance in order that they are ready when you need them. Cut the pork into pieces about ³/₄ inch/2 cm square and put in a large, shallow, nonmetallic dish that will hold the pieces in a single layer.

To prepare the marinade, put all the remaining ingredients in a bowl and mix well together. Pour the marinade over the pork and toss the meat in it until well coated. Cover the dish and let marinate in the refrigerator for 8 hours or overnight, stirring the pork 2–3 times.

You can use wooden or metal skewers to cook the brochettes and for this recipe you will need about 12 x 6-inch/15-cm skewers.

If you are using wooden ones, soak them in cold water for about 30 minutes prior to using. This helps to stop them burning and the food sticking to them during cooking. Metal skewers simply need to be greased, and flat ones should be used in preference to round ones to prevent the food on them falling off.

Preheat the broiler, grill pan, or barbecue. Thread 3 marinated pork pieces, leaving a little space between each piece, onto each prepared skewer. Cook the brochettes for 10–15 minutes, or until tender and lightly charred, turning several times and basting with the remaining marinade during cooking. Serve the pork brochettes piping hot, garnished with parsley.

MAKES 12

1 lb/450 g lean boneless pork

3 tbsp Spanish olive oil, plus extra for oiling (optional)

grated rind and juice of 1 large lemon

2 garlic cloves, crushed

2 tbsp chopped fresh flat-leaf parsley, plus extra to garnish

1 tbsp ras-el-hanout Moroccan spice blend

salt and pepper

COD & CAPER CROQUETTES

MAKES 12

12 oz/350 g whitefish fillets, such as cod, haddock, or monkfish

1¹/₄ cups milk

salt and pepper

4 tbsp Spanish olive oil or 2 oz/55 g butter

scant ¹/₂ cup all-purpose flour, plus extra to flour hands

4 tbsp capers, coarsely chopped

1 tsp paprika

1 garlic clove, crushed

1 tsp lemon juice

3 tbsp chopped fresh flat-leaf parsley, plus extra sprigs to garnish

1 egg, beaten

1 cup fresh white bread crumbs

1 tbsp sesame seeds

corn oil, for deep-frying

lemon wedges, to garnish

mayonnaise, to serve

Put the fish fillets in a large, heavy-bottom skillet. Pour in the milk and season to taste with salt and pepper. Bring to a boil, then lower the heat, cover the skillet, and let simmer gently for 8–10 minutes, or until the fish flakes easily when tested with a fork. Using a spatula, remove the fish fillets from the skillet. Pour the milk into a pitcher and set aside for later. Flake the fish, removing and discarding any skin and bones.

Heat the olive oil or butter in a pan. Stir in the flour to form a paste and cook gently, stirring, for 1 minute. Remove the pan from the heat and gradually stir in the reserved milk until smooth. Return to the heat and slowly bring to a boil, stirring all the time, until the mixture thickens.

Remove the pan from the heat, add the flaked fish, and beat until the mixture is smooth. Add the capers, paprika, garlic, lemon juice, and parsley and mix well together. Season the mixture to taste with salt and pepper. Spread the fish mixture in a dish and let stand until cool, then cover and put in the refrigerator for 2–3 hours or overnight.

When the fish mixture has chilled, pour the beaten egg onto a plate. Put the bread crumbs and sesame seeds on a separate plate, mix together, and spread out. Divide the fish mixture into 12 equal-size portions. Then, with lightly floured hands, form each portion into a sausage shape, measuring about 3 inches/7.5 cm in length. Dip the croquettes, one at a time, in the beaten egg, then roll in the bread crumb mixture to coat them. Place on a plate and let chill for about 1 hour.

To cook the croquettes, heat the oil in a deep-fryer to 350–375°F/180–190°C, or until a cube of bread browns in 30 seconds. Add the croquettes, in batches, and deep-fry for 3 minutes, or until golden brown and crispy. Remove from the pan with a slotted spoon and drain well on paper towels.

Serve piping hot, garnished with lemon wedges and parsley sprigs, and accompanied by a bowl of mayonnaise for dipping.

CHICKEN IN LEMON AND GARLIC

Using a sharp knife, slice the chicken breasts widthwise into very thin slices. Heat the olive oil in a large, heavy-bottom skillet, add the onion and cook for 5 minutes, or until softened but not browned. Add the garlic and cook for an additional 30 seconds.

Add the sliced chicken to the skillet and cook gently for 5–10 minutes, stirring from time to time, until all the ingredients are lightly browned and the chicken is tender.

Add the grated lemon rind and the lemon juice and let it bubble. At the same time, deglaze the skillet by scraping and stirring all the bits on the bottom of the skillet into the juices with a wooden spoon. Remove the skillet from the heat, stir in the parsley, and season to taste with salt and pepper.

Transfer the chicken in lemon and garlic, piping hot, to a warmed serving dish. Sprinkle with the pared lemon rind, garnish with the parsley, and serve with lemon wedges for squeezing over the chicken, accompanied by chunks or slices of crusty bread for mopping up the lemon and garlic juices.

**SERVES 6–8
as part of a tapas
meal**

4 large skinless,
boneless chicken
breasts

5 tbsp Spanish olive oil

1 onion, finely chopped

6 garlic cloves, finely
chopped

grated rind of 1 lemon,
finely pared rind of
1 lemon and juice of
both lemons

4 tbsp chopped fresh
flat-leaf parsley, plus
extra to garnish

salt and pepper

lemon wedges and
crusty bread, to serve

CALAMARI

SERVES 6
as part of a tapas meal

1 lb/450 g
cleaned squid

all-purpose flour,
for coating

corn oil, for deep-frying

salt

lemon wedges,
to garnish

Aïoli (see page 164),
to serve

Slice the squid into ½-inch/1-cm rings and halve the tentacles if large. Rinse and dry well on paper towels so that they do not spit during cooking. Dust the squid rings with flour so that they are lightly coated. Do not season the flour, as Spanish cooks will tell you that seasoning squid with salt before cooking toughens it. They should know!

Heat the corn oil in a deep-fryer to 350–375°F/180–190°C, or until a cube of bread browns in 30 seconds. Carefully add the squid rings, in batches so that the temperature of the oil does not drop, and deep-fry for 2–3 minutes, or until golden brown and crisp all over, turning several times. Do not overcook as the squid will become tough and rubbery rather than moist and tender.

Using a slotted spoon, remove the deep-fried squid from the deep-fryer and drain well on paper towels. Transfer to a warm oven while you deep-fry the remaining squid rings.

Sprinkle the deep-fried squid with salt and serve piping hot, garnished with lemon wedges for squeezing over them. Accompany with a bowl of Aïoli in which to dip the pieces.

CRISPY CHICKEN & HAM CROQUETTES

Heat the olive oil or butter in a pan. Stir in the flour to form a paste and cook gently for 1 minute, stirring constantly. Remove the pan from the heat and gradually stir in the milk until smooth. Return to the heat and slowly bring to a boil, stirring all the time, until the mixture boils and thickens.

Remove the pan from the heat, add the ground chicken, and beat until the mixture is smooth. Add the chopped ham, parsley, and nutmeg and mix well together. Season the mixture to taste with salt and pepper. Spread the chicken mixture in a dish and let stand for 30 minutes, until cool, then cover and put in the refrigerator for 2–3 hours or overnight. Don't be tempted to miss out this stage, as chilling helps to stop the croquettes from falling apart when they are cooked.

When the chicken mixture has chilled, pour the beaten egg onto a plate and spread out the bread crumbs on a separate plate. Divide the chicken mixture into 8 equal-size portions. With dampened hands, form each portion into a cylindrical shape. Dip the croquettes, one at a time, in the beaten egg, then roll in the bread crumbs to coat them. Place on a plate and let chill in the refrigerator for about 1 hour.

To cook the croquettes, heat the oil in a deep-fryer to 350–375°F/180–190°C, or until a cube of bread browns in 30 seconds. Add the croquettes, in batches to prevent the temperature of the oil from dropping, and deep-fry for 5–10 minutes, or until golden brown and crispy. Remove from the pan with a slotted spoon and drain well on paper towels.

Serve the croquettes piping hot, garnished with parsley sprigs, and accompanied by a bowl of Aïoli for dipping.

MAKES 8

4 tbsp Spanish olive oil or 2 oz/55 g butter

4 tbsp all-purpose flour

scant 1 cup milk

4 oz/115 g cooked chicken, ground

2 oz/55 g serrano or cooked ham, very finely chopped

1 tbsp chopped fresh flat-leaf parsley, plus extra sprigs to garnish

small pinch of freshly grated nutmeg

salt and pepper

1 egg, beaten

1 cup day-old white bread crumbs

corn oil, for deep-frying

Aïoli (see page 164), to serve

LIME-DRIZZLED SHRIMP

**SERVES 6
as part of a tapas
meal**

4 limes

12 raw jumbo shrimp,
in their shells

3 tbsp Spanish olive oil

2 garlic cloves, finely
chopped

splash of fino sherry

salt and pepper

4 tbsp chopped fresh
flat-leaf parsley

Grate the rind and squeeze the juice from 2 of the limes. Cut the remaining 2 limes into wedges and set aside for later.

To prepare the shrimp, remove the heads and legs, leaving the shells and tails intact. Using a sharp knife, make a shallow slit along the back of each shrimp, then pull out the dark vein and discard. Rinse the shrimp under cold water and dry well on paper towels.

Heat the olive oil in a large, heavy-bottom skillet, then add the garlic and cook for 30 seconds. Add the shrimp and cook for 5 minutes, stirring from time to time, or until they turn pink and start to curl. Mix in the lime rind, juice, and a splash of sherry to moisten, then stir well together.

Transfer the cooked shrimp to a serving dish, season to taste with salt and pepper, and sprinkle with the parsley. Serve piping hot, accompanied by the reserved lime wedges for squeezing over the shrimp.

FAVA BEANS WITH SERRANO HAM

Using a sharp knife, cut the ham, pancetta, or bacon into small strips. Cut the chorizo into ¾-inch/2-cm cubes. Heat the olive oil in a large, heavy-bottom skillet or ovenproof dish that has a lid. Add the onion and cook for 5 minutes, or until softened and starting to brown. If you are using pancetta or bacon, add it with the onion. Add the garlic and cook for 30 seconds.

Pour the wine into the skillet, increase the heat, and let it bubble to evaporate the alcohol, then lower the heat. Add the fava beans, ham, if using, and the chorizo and cook for 1–2 minutes, stirring all the time to coat in the oil.

Cover the skillet and let the beans simmer very gently in the oil, stirring from time to time, for 10–15 minutes, or until the beans are tender. It may be necessary to add a little water to the skillet during cooking, so keep an eye on it and add a splash if the beans appear to become too dry. Stir in the mint or dill and sugar. Season the dish with salt and pepper, but taste first as you may find that it does not need any salt.

Transfer the fava beans to a large, warmed serving dish, several smaller ones, or individual plates and serve piping hot, garnished with chopped mint or dill.

**SERVES 6–8
as part of a tapas
meal**

2 oz/55 g serrano ham
or prosciutto, pancetta,
or rindless smoked
lean bacon

4 oz/115 g chorizo
sausage, outer casing
removed

4 tbsp Spanish olive oil

1 onion, finely chopped

2 garlic cloves, finely
chopped

splash of dry white
wine

1 lb/450 g frozen fava
beans, thawed,
or about 3 lb/1.3 kg
fresh fava beans in
their pods, shelled to
give 1 lb/450 g

1 tbsp chopped fresh
mint or dill, plus extra
to garnish

pinch of sugar

salt and pepper

TUNA WITH PIMIENTO-STUFFED OLIVES

**SERVES 6
as part of a tapas
meal**

2 fresh tuna steaks,
weighing about
9 oz/250 g in total and
about 1 inch/2.5 cm
thick

5 tbsp Spanish olive oil

3 tbsp red wine vinegar

4 sprigs of fresh thyme,
plus extra to garnish

1 bay leaf

salt and pepper

2 tbsp all-purpose flour

1 onion, finely chopped

2 garlic cloves, finely
chopped

1/2 cup pimiento-
stuffed green olives,
sliced

crusty bread, to serve

Don't get caught out with this recipe—the tuna steaks need to be marinated, so remember to start preparing the dish the day before you are going to serve it. Remove any skin from the tuna steaks, then cut the steaks in half along the grain of the fish. Cut each half into 1/2-inch/1-cm thick slices against the grain.

Put 3 tablespoons of the olive oil and the vinegar in a large, shallow, nonmetallic dish. Strip the leaves from the sprigs of thyme and add these to the dish with the bay leaf and salt and pepper to taste. Add the prepared strips of tuna, cover the dish, and let marinate in the refrigerator for 8 hours or overnight.

The next day, put the flour in a plastic bag. Remove the tuna strips from the marinade, reserving the marinade for later, add them to the bag of flour and toss well until they are lightly coated.

Heat the remaining olive oil in a large, heavy-bottom skillet. Add the onion and garlic and gently cook for 5–10 minutes, or until softened and golden brown. Add the tuna strips to the skillet and cook for 2–5 minutes, turning several times, until the fish becomes opaque. Add the reserved marinade and olives to the skillet and cook for an additional 1–2 minutes, stirring, until the fish is tender and the sauce has thickened.

Serve the tuna and olives piping hot, garnished with thyme sprigs. Accompany with chunks or slices of crusty bread for mopping up the sauce.

ROASTED ASPARAGUS WITH MOUNTAIN HAM

Preheat the oven to 400°F/200°C. Put half the olive oil in a roasting pan that will hold the asparagus spears in a single layer and swirl it around so that it covers the bottom. Cut each slice of serrano ham in half lengthwise.

Trim the ends of the asparagus spears, then wrap a slice of ham around the stem end of each spear. Place the wrapped spears in the prepared roasting pan and lightly brush the ham and asparagus with the remaining olive oil. Season the spears with pepper.

Roast the asparagus spears in the oven for 10 minutes, depending on the thickness of the asparagus, or until tender but still firm. Do not overcook the asparagus spears as it is important that they are still firm.

Serve piping hot, accompanied by a bowl of Aïoli for dipping.

MAKES 12

2 tbsp Spanish olive oil

6 slices serrano ham

12 asparagus spears

pepper

Aïoli (see page 164), to serve

MONKFISH, ROSEMARY & BACON SKEWERS

MAKES 12

12 oz/350 g monkfish tail or 9 oz/250 g monkfish fillet

12 stalks of fresh rosemary

3 tbsp Spanish olive oil

juice of ¹/₂ small lemon

1 garlic clove, crushed

salt and pepper

6 thick slices Canadian bacon

lemon wedges, to garnish

Aïoli (see page 164), to serve

If using monkfish tail, cut either side of the central bone with a sharp knife and remove the flesh to form 2 fillets. Slice the fillets in half lengthwise, then cut each fillet into 12 bite-size chunks to give a total of 24 pieces. Put the monkfish pieces in a large bowl.

To prepare the rosemary skewers, strip the leaves off the stalks and set them aside, leaving a few leaves at one end.

For the marinade, finely chop the reserved leaves and whisk together in a bowl with the olive oil, lemon juice, garlic, and salt and pepper to taste. Add the monkfish pieces and toss until coated in the marinade. Cover and let marinate in the refrigerator for 1–2 hours.

Cut each bacon slice in half lengthwise, then in half widthwise, and roll up each piece.

Thread 2 pieces of monkfish alternately with 2 bacon rolls onto the prepared rosemary skewers.

Preheat the broiler, grill pan, or barbecue. If you are cooking the skewers under a broiler, arrange them on the broiler pan so that the leaves of the rosemary skewers protrude from the broiler and therefore do not catch fire during cooking. Broil the monkfish and bacon skewers for 10 minutes, turning from time to time and basting with any remaining marinade, or until cooked. Serve hot, garnished with lemon wedges for squeezing over them and accompanied by a bowl of Aïoli in which to dip them.

BEEF SKEWERS WITH ORANGE & GARLIC

Mix the wine, olive oil, garlic, and orange juice together in a shallow, nonmetallic dish. Add the cubes of steak, season to taste with salt and pepper, and toss to coat. Cover with plastic wrap and let marinate in the refrigerator for 2–8 hours.

Preheat the broiler to high. Drain the steak, reserving the marinade. Thread the steak, onions, bell peppers, and tomatoes alternately onto several small skewers.

Cook the skewers under the hot broiler, turning and brushing frequently with the marinade, for 10 minutes, or until cooked through. Transfer to warmed serving plates and serve immediately.

**SERVES 6–8
as part of a tapas
meal**

3 tbsp white wine

2 tbsp Spanish olive oil

3 garlic cloves, finely
chopped

juice of 1 orange

1 lb/450 g rump steak,
cubed

1 lb/450 g pearl onions,
halved

2 orange bell peppers,
seeded and cut into
squares

8 oz/225 g cherry
tomatoes, halved

salt and pepper

DEEP-FRIED SARDINES

**SERVES 6–8
as part of a tapas
meal**

¹/₂ cup red wine
vinegar

3 garlic cloves,
finely chopped

1 fresh red chile,
seeded and finely
chopped

2 tbsp chopped fresh
parsley

2 lb 4 oz/1 kg fresh
sardines, scaled,
cleaned, and heads
removed

generous ³/₄ cup
all-purpose flour

vegetable oil, for
deep-frying

salt and pepper

lemon wedges,
to garnish

Mix the vinegar, garlic, chile, and parsley together in a nonmetallic dish. Add the sardines and turn to coat. Cover with plastic wrap and let marinate in the refrigerator for 1 hour.

Drain the sardines and pat dry with paper towels. Place the flour in a plastic bag and season to taste with salt and pepper. Add the sardines, a few at a time, shaking to coat well.

Heat the vegetable oil in a deep-fryer or large pan to 350–375°F/180–190°C, or until a cube of bread browns in 30 seconds. Deep-fry the sardines, in batches, for 4–5 minutes, or until golden brown. Remove and drain on paper towels. Keep warm while you cook the remaining sardines. Serve garnished with lemon wedges.

LAMB SKEWERS WITH LEMON

Mix the garlic, onion, lemon rind, lemon juice, thyme, coriander, cumin, vinegar, and olive oil together in a large, shallow, nonmetallic dish, whisking well until thoroughly combined.

Thread the pieces of lamb onto 16 wooden skewers and add to the dish, turning well to coat. Cover with plastic wrap and let marinate in the refrigerator for 2–8 hours, turning occasionally.

Preheat the broiler to medium. Drain the skewers, reserving the marinade. Cook under the hot broiler, turning frequently and brushing with the marinade for 10 minutes, or until tender and cooked to your liking. Serve immediately, garnished with orange or lemon slices.

**SERVES 8
as part of a tapas
meal**

2 garlic cloves, finely
chopped

1 Spanish or Bermuda
onion, finely chopped

2 tsp finely grated
lemon rind

2 tbsp lemon juice

1 tsp fresh thyme
leaves

1 tsp ground coriander

1 tsp ground cumin

2 tbsp red wine vinegar

$^1/_2$ cup Spanish olive oil

2 lb 4 oz/1 kg lamb
fillet, cut into
$^3/_4$-inch/2-cm pieces

orange or lemon slices,
to garnish

MUSSELS WITH HERB & GARLIC BUTTER

**SERVES 8
as part of a tapas
meal**

1 lb 12 oz/800 g fresh
mussels, in their shells

splash of dry white wine

1 bay leaf

6 tbsp/85 g butter

generous ¹/₂ cup fresh
white or brown bread
crumbs

4 tbsp chopped fresh
flat-leaf parsley, plus
extra sprigs to garnish

2 tbsp snipped fresh
chives

2 garlic cloves, finely
chopped

salt and pepper

lemon wedges, to
serve

Clean the mussels by scrubbing or scraping the shells and pulling out any beards that are attached to them. Discard any with broken shells and any that refuse to close when tapped. Put the mussels in a strainer and rinse well under cold running water. Preheat the oven to 450°F/230°C.

Put the mussels in a large pan and add a splash of wine and the bay leaf. Cook, covered, over high heat for 5 minutes, shaking the pan occasionally, or until the mussels are opened. Drain the mussels and discard any that remain closed.

Shell the mussels, reserving one half of each shell. Arrange the mussels, in their half shells, in a large, shallow, ovenproof serving dish.

Melt the butter and pour into a small bowl. Add the bread crumbs, parsley, chives, garlic, and salt and pepper to taste and mix well together. Let stand until the butter has set slightly. Using your fingers or 2 teaspoons, take a large pinch of the herb and butter mixture and use to fill each mussel shell, pressing it down well. You can chill the filled mussels in the refrigerator at this point until ready to serve.

To serve, bake the mussels in the oven for 10 minutes, or until hot. Serve immediately, garnished with parsley sprigs, and accompanied by lemon wedges to squeeze over them.

CHORIZO & MUSHROOM KABOBS

Heat the olive oil in a skillet over medium heat. Add the chorizo and cook for 20 seconds, stirring.

Add the mushrooms and continue cooking for an additional 1–2 minutes until the mushrooms begin to brown and absorb the fat in the skillet.

Thread a bell pepper square, a piece of chorizo, and a mushroom onto a wooden toothpick. Continue until all the ingredients are used. Serve hot or at room temperature.

MAKES 25

2 tbsp Spanish olive oil

25 pieces chorizo sausage, each about $^1/_2$-inch/1-cm square (about $3^1/_2$ oz/100 g)

25 white mushrooms, wiped and stems removed

1 green bell pepper, broiled, peeled, and cut into 5 squares

SHRIMP WRAPPED IN HAM

MAKES 16

16 raw jumbo shrimp

16 thin slices serrano ham or prosciutto

extra virgin Spanish olive oil

TOMATO-CAPER DRESSING

2 tomatoes, peeled and seeded

1 small red onion, very finely chopped

4 tbsp very finely chopped fresh parsley

1 tbsp capers in brine, drained, rinsed, and chopped

finely grated rind of 1 large lemon

4 tbsp extra virgin Spanish olive oil

1 tbsp sherry vinegar

Preheat the oven to 325°F/160°C. To make the dressing, finely chop the prepared tomato flesh and place in a bowl. Add the onion, parsley, capers, and lemon rind and gently toss together. Combine the olive oil and vinegar and add to the other ingredients. Reserve until required.

Pull the heads off the shrimp and peel, leaving the tails intact. Cut along the length of the back of each shrimp and remove and discard the dark vein. Rinse and pat dry. Wrap a slice of ham around each shrimp and rub with a little oil. Place the shrimp in a heatproof dish large enough to hold them in a single layer. Bake in the preheated oven for 10 minutes.

Transfer the shrimp to a serving platter and spoon the dressing over or serve it in a bowl on the side. Serve immediately, or let cool to room temperature.

Spanish Sauces & Dips

FRESH SALMON IN MOJO SAUCE

**SERVES 8
as part of a tapas
meal**

4 fresh salmon fillets,
weighing about
1 lb 10 oz/750 g
in total

3 tbsp Spanish olive oil

1 fresh flat-leaf parsley
sprig, to garnish

MOJO SAUCE

2 garlic cloves, peeled

2 tsp paprika

1 tsp ground cumin

5 tbsp Spanish extra
virgin olive oil

2 tbsp white wine
vinegar

salt and pepper

To prepare the Mojo Sauce, put the garlic, paprika, and cumin in the bowl of a food processor fitted with the metal blade and, using a pulsing action, blend for 1 minute to mix well together. With the motor still running, add 1 tablespoon of the olive oil, drop by drop, through the feeder tube. When it has been added, scrape down the sides of the bowl with a spatula, then very slowly continue to pour in the oil in a thin, steady stream, until all the oil has been added and the sauce has slightly thickened. Add the vinegar and blend for an additional 1 minute. Season the sauce with salt to taste.

To prepare the salmon, remove the skin, cut each fillet in half widthwise, then cut lengthwise into $^3/_4$-inch/2-cm thick slices, discarding any bones. Season the pieces of fish to taste with salt and pepper.

Heat the olive oil in a large, heavy-bottom skillet. When hot, add the pieces of fish and cook for about 10 minutes, depending on their thickness, turning occasionally until cooked and browned on both sides.

Transfer the salmon to a warmed serving dish, drizzle over some of the Mojo Sauce, and serve hot, garnished with parsley, and accompanied by the remaining sauce in a small serving bowl.

ZUCCHINI FRITTERS WITH A DIPPING SAUCE

If you have chosen to serve the pine nut sauce with the zucchini fritters, then make this first. Put the pine nuts and garlic in a food processor and blend to form a purée. With the motor still running, gradually add the olive oil, lemon juice, and water to form a smooth sauce. Stir in the parsley and season to taste with salt and pepper. Turn into a serving bowl.

To prepare the zucchini, cut them on the diagonal into thin slices about 1/4 inch/5 mm thick. Put the flour and paprika in a plastic bag and mix together. Beat the egg and milk together in a large bowl.

Add the zucchini slices to the flour mixture and toss well together until coated. Shake off the excess flour. Pour enough corn oil into a large, heavy-bottom skillet for a depth of about 1/2 inch/1 cm, and heat. Dip the zucchini slices, one at a time, into the egg mixture, then slip them into the hot oil. Cook the zucchini slices, in batches of a single layer so that they do not overcrowd the skillet, for 2 minutes, or until crisp and golden brown.

Using a slotted spoon, remove the zucchini fritters from the skillet and drain on paper towels. Continue until all the zucchini slices have been cooked.

Serve the zucchini fritters piping hot, lightly sprinkled with sea salt. Accompany with a bowl of your chosen dipping sauce, garnished with dill.

**SERVES 8
as part of a tapas meal**

1 lb/450 g small zucchini

3 tbsp all-purpose flour

1 tsp paprika

1 large egg

2 tbsp milk

corn oil, for pan-frying

coarse sea salt

dipping sauce such as Aïoli (see page 164) or the Pine Nut Sauce (see below)

PINE NUT SAUCE

generous 1/2 cup pine nuts

1 garlic clove, peeled

3 tbsp Spanish extra virgin olive oil

1 tbsp lemon juice

3 tbsp water

1 tbsp chopped fresh flat-leaf parsley

salt and pepper

dill sprig, to garnish

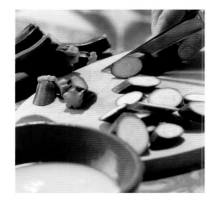

NEW POTATOES WITH CHILE SAUCE

Place the potatoes in a steamer set over a pan of boiling water. Cover and steam for 30 minutes, or until tender.

Meanwhile, make the sauce. Place the garlic, chiles, and paprika in a mortar and grind to a paste with a pestle. Season to taste with salt, then gradually work in the vinegar. Finally, work in the olive oil.

Transfer the potatoes to warmed serving dishes and serve immediately, handing round the chile sauce separately. Provide toothpicks for picking up and dipping the potatoes.

**SERVES 4–6
as part of a tapas
meal**

1 lb/450 g new
potatoes, unpeeled

2 garlic cloves, chopped

2 dried red chiles,
lightly crushed

1 tbsp paprika

2 tbsp sherry vinegar

2/3 cup Spanish olive oil

salt

GREEN BEANS IN TOMATO SAUCE

Melt the butter in a large, heavy-bottom skillet. Add the garlic and scallions and cook over medium heat, stirring occasionally, for 3–4 minutes. Add the beans and cook, stirring frequently, for an additional 4 minutes.

Add the tomatoes with their can juices, pine nuts, lemon juice, and bay leaf, and season to taste with salt and pepper. Reduce the heat and let simmer gently for 30 minutes, or until the beans are tender and the sauce is pulpy.

Remove and discard the bay leaf. Taste and adjust the seasoning if necessary. Transfer to warmed serving dishes and serve hot.

**SERVES 6
as part of a tapas
meal**

2 tbsp butter

2 garlic cloves,
finely chopped

2 scallions,
finely chopped

2 lb 4 oz/1 kg green
beans, cut into
1-inch/2.5-cm lengths

1 lb 9 oz/700 g canned
chopped tomatoes

1 tbsp pine nuts

1 tbsp lemon juice

1 bay leaf

salt and pepper

BATTERED SHRIMP & CILANTRO DIP

SERVES 4
as part of a tapas meal

12 raw shrimp

1 egg

1/2 cup water

generous 3/4 cup all-purpose flour

1 tsp cayenne pepper

vegetable oil, for deep-frying

orange wedges, to garnish

CILANTRO DIP

1 large bunch of cilantro, coarsely chopped

3 garlic cloves, chopped

2 tbsp tomato paste

2 tbsp lemon juice

1 tbsp grated lemon rind

1 1/2 tbsp sugar

1 tsp ground cumin

5 tbsp Spanish olive oil

First make the cilantro dip. Place the cilantro, garlic, tomato paste, lemon juice, lemon rind, sugar, and cumin in a food processor or blender and process until combined. With the motor still running, gradually add the olive oil through the feeder tube until fully incorporated. Scrape into a bowl, then cover with plastic wrap and let chill until required.

Pull the heads off the shrimp and peel, leaving the tails intact. Cut along the length of the back of each shrimp and remove and discard the dark vein. Rinse under cold running water, then pat dry with paper towels.

Whisk the egg with the water in a small bowl. Gradually sift in the flour and cayenne, whisking constantly until smooth.

Heat the vegetable oil in a deep-fryer or large pan to 350–375°F/180–190°C, or until a cube of bread browns in 30 seconds. Holding the shrimp by their tails, dip them into the batter, one at a time, shaking off any excess. Add the shrimp to the oil and deep-fry for 2–3 minutes, or until crisp. Remove with a slotted spoon and drain well on paper towels. Serve immediately, garnished with orange wedges. Hand round the cilantro dip separately.

TINY SPANISH MEATBALLS IN ALMOND SAUCE

To prepare the meatballs, put the bread in a bowl, add the water, and let soak for 5 minutes. With your hands, squeeze out the water and return the bread to the dried bowl. Add the pork, onion, garlic, parsley, and egg, then season generously with grated nutmeg and a little salt and pepper. Knead the ingredients well together to form a smooth mixture.

Spread some flour on a plate. With floured hands, shape the meat mixture into about 30 equal-size balls, then roll each meatball in flour until coated.

Heat the olive oil in a large, heavy-bottom skillet, add the meatballs, in batches so that they do not overcrowd the skillet, and cook for 4–5 minutes, or until browned on all sides. Using a slotted spoon, remove the meatballs from the skillet and set aside.

To make the Almond Sauce, heat the olive oil in the same skillet in which the meatballs were cooked. Break the bread into small pieces, add to the skillet with the almonds and cook gently, stirring frequently, until the bread and almonds are golden brown. Add the garlic and cook for an additional 30 seconds, then pour in the wine and boil for 1–2 minutes. Season to taste with salt and pepper and let cool slightly.

Transfer the almond mixture to a food processor. Pour in the vegetable stock and blend the mixture until smooth. Return the sauce to the skillet.

Carefully add the cooked meatballs to the almond sauce and let simmer for 25 minutes, or until the meatballs are tender. Taste the sauce and season with salt and pepper if necessary.

Transfer the cooked meatballs and almond sauce to a warmed serving dish, then add a squeeze of lemon juice to taste and sprinkle with chopped parsley to garnish. Serve piping hot, accompanied by chunks or slices of crusty bread for mopping up the Almond Sauce.

**SERVES 6–8
as part of a tapas meal**

2 oz/55 g white or brown bread, crusts removed

3 tbsp water

2 cups fresh lean ground pork

1 large onion, finely chopped

1 garlic clove, crushed

2 tbsp chopped fresh flat-leaf parsley, plus extra to garnish

1 egg, beaten

freshly grated nutmeg

flour, for coating

2 tbsp Spanish olive oil

squeeze of lemon juice

crusty bread, to serve

salt and pepper

ALMOND SAUCE

2 tbsp Spanish olive oil

1 oz/25 g white or brown bread

$2/3$ cup blanched almonds

2 garlic cloves, finely chopped

$2/3$ cup dry white wine

scant 2 cups vegetable stock

salt and pepper

EGGPLANT & BELL PEPPER DIP

**SERVES 6–8
as part of a tapas
meal**

2 large eggplants

2 red bell peppers

4 tbsp Spanish olive oil

2 garlic cloves,
coarsely chopped

grated rind and juice of
$1/2$ lemon

1 tbsp chopped fresh
cilantro, plus extra
sprigs to garnish

$1/2$–1 tsp paprika

salt and pepper

bread or toast, to serve

Preheat the oven to 375°F/190°C. Prick the skins of the eggplants and bell peppers all over with a fork and brush with about 1 tablespoon of the olive oil. Put on a baking sheet and bake in the oven for 45 minutes, or until the skins are starting to turn black, the flesh of the eggplant is very soft, and the bell peppers are deflated.

When the vegetables are cooked, put them in a bowl and immediately cover tightly with a clean, damp dish towel. Alternatively, you can put the vegetables in a plastic bag. Let them stand for about 15 minutes, until they are cool enough to handle.

When the vegetables have cooled, cut the eggplants in half lengthwise, carefully scoop out the flesh, and discard the skin. Cut the eggplant flesh into large chunks. Remove and discard the stem, core, and seeds from the bell peppers and cut the flesh into large pieces.

Heat the remaining olive oil in a large, heavy-bottom skillet, add the eggplant flesh and bell pepper pieces and cook for 5 minutes. Add the garlic and cook for an additional 30 seconds.

Turn all the contents of the skillet onto paper towels to drain, then transfer to the bowl of a food processor. Add the lemon rind and juice, the chopped cilantro, the paprika, and salt and pepper according to taste, and blend until a speckled purée is formed.

Turn the eggplant and bell pepper dip into a serving bowl. Serve warm, at room temperature, or let cool for 30 minutes, then let chill in the refrigerator for at least 1 hour and serve cold. Garnish with cilantro sprigs and accompany with thick slices of bread or toast for dipping.

CHEESE PUFFS WITH FIERY TOMATO SALSA

To make the salsa, heat the olive oil in a pan, add the onion and cook for 5 minutes, or until softened but not browned. Add the garlic and cook for an additional 30 seconds. Add the wine and let bubble, then add all the remaining salsa ingredients to the pan and let simmer, uncovered, for 10–15 minutes, or until a thick sauce is formed. Spoon into a serving bowl and set aside until ready to serve.

Meanwhile, prepare the cheese puffs. Sift the flour onto a plate or sheet of waxed paper. Put the olive oil and water in a pan and slowly bring to a boil. As soon as the water boils, remove the pan from the heat, and quickly tip in the flour all at once. Using a wooden spoon, beat the mixture well until it is smooth and leaves the sides of the pan.

Let the mixture cool for 1–2 minutes, then gradually add the eggs, beating hard after each addition and keeping the mixture stiff. Add the cheese and paprika, season to taste with salt and pepper, and mix well together. You can store the mixture in the refrigerator at this stage until you are ready to deep-fry the cheese puffs.

Just before serving the cheese puffs, heat the corn oil in a deep-fryer to 350–375°F/ 180–190°C, or until a cube of bread browns in 30 seconds. Drop teaspoonfuls of the prepared mixture, in batches, into the hot oil and deep-fry for 2–3 minutes, turning once, or until golden and crispy. They should rise to the surface of the oil and puff up. Drain well on paper towels.

Serve the puffs piping hot, accompanied by the fiery salsa for dipping, and toothpicks to spear the puffs.

SERVES 8
as part of a tapas meal

scant ¹/₂ cup all-purpose flour

¹/₄ cup Spanish olive oil

²/₃ cup water

2 eggs, beaten

¹/₂ cup Manchego, Parmesan, Cheddar, Gouda, or Gruyère cheese, finely grated

¹/₂ tsp paprika

corn oil, for deep-frying

FIERY TOMATO SALSA

2 tbsp Spanish olive oil

1 small onion, finely chopped

1 garlic clove, crushed

splash of dry white wine

14 oz/400 g canned chopped tomatoes

1 tbsp tomato paste

¹/₄–¹/₂ tsp dried red chile flakes

dash of Tabasco sauce

pinch of sugar

salt and pepper

BABY POTATOES WITH AÏOLI

**SERVES 6–8
as part of a tapas
meal**

1 lb/450 g baby new
potatoes

1 tbsp chopped fresh
flat-leaf parsley

AÏOLI

1 large egg yolk, at
room temperature

1 tbsp white wine
vinegar or lemon juice

2 large garlic cloves,
peeled

5 tbsp Spanish extra
virgin olive oil

5 tbsp corn oil

salt and pepper

To make the Aïoli, put the egg yolk, vinegar, garlic, and salt and pepper to taste in the bowl of a food processor fitted with the metal blade and blend well together. With the motor still running, very slowly add the olive oil, then the corn oil, drop by drop at first, then, when it starts to thicken, in a slow, steady stream until the sauce is thick and smooth. Alternatively, mix in a bowl with a whisk.

For this recipe, the Aïoli should be a little thin so that it coats the potatoes. To ensure this, quickly blend in 1 tablespoon water so that it forms the consistency of sauce.

To prepare the potatoes, cut them in half or quarters to make bite-size pieces. If they are very small, you can leave them whole. Put the potatoes in a large pan of cold, salted water and bring to a boil. Lower the heat and let simmer for 7 minutes, or until just tender. Drain well, then turn out into a large bowl.

While the potatoes are still warm, pour over the Aïoli sauce, and gently toss the potatoes in it. Adding the sauce to the potatoes while they are still warm will help them to absorb the garlic flavor. Let stand for about 20 minutes to allow the potatoes to marinate in the sauce.

Transfer the potatoes with Aïoli to a warmed serving dish, sprinkle over the parsley and salt to taste, and serve warm. Alternatively, the Aïoli can be served separately, allowing diners to dip the potatoes themselves.

STEAK BITES WITH CHILE SAUCE

Heat half the olive oil in a heavy-bottom saucepan. Add the onion and cook over low heat, stirring occasionally, for 5 minutes, or until softened. Add the paprika, garlic, and chile and cook for an additional 2–3 minutes, then stir in the tomatoes with their juices, wine, tomato paste, vinegar, and sugar. Simmer gently for 15–20 minutes, or until thickened.

Meanwhile, heat a heavy-bottom skillet or grill pan over high heat and brush with the remaining olive oil. Season the steaks to taste with pepper and rub with the Tabasco, then add to the pan. Cook for 1–1½ minutes on each side, or until browned. Reduce the heat and cook, turning once, for 3 minutes for rare, 4–5 minutes for medium, or 5–7 minutes for well done. Remove from the heat and keep warm.

Transfer the sauce to a food processor or blender and process until fairly smooth. Transfer to a serving bowl, then season to taste with salt and pepper and stir in the parsley.

Transfer the steaks to a cutting board and cut into bite-size pieces. Spear with wooden toothpicks, then place on serving plates and serve immediately with the sauce.

SERVES 4–6
as part of a tapas meal

2 tbsp Spanish olive oil

1 onion, chopped

1 tsp paprika

1 garlic clove, finely chopped

1 fresh red chile, seeded and sliced

14 oz/400 g canned chopped tomatoes

2 tbsp dry white wine

1 tbsp tomato paste

1 tbsp sherry vinegar

2 tsp sugar

2 rump steaks, about 6–8 oz/175–225 g each

2 tsp Tabasco sauce

1 tbsp chopped fresh parsley

salt and pepper

CHICKEN LIVERS IN SHERRY SAUCE

**SERVES 6
as part of a tapas
meal**

1 lb/450 g chicken
livers

2 tbsp Spanish olive oil

1 small onion, finely
chopped

2 garlic cloves, finely
chopped

generous $^1/_3$ cup dry
Spanish sherry

2 tbsp chopped fresh
flat-leaf parsley

salt and pepper

crusty bread or toast,
to serve

If necessary, trim the chicken livers, cutting away any ducts and gristle, then cut them into small, bite-size pieces.

Heat the olive oil in a large, heavy-bottom skillet. Add the onion and cook for 5 minutes, or until softened but not browned. Add the garlic and cook for an additional 30 seconds.

Add the chicken livers to the skillet and cook for 2–3 minutes, stirring all the time, until they are firm and have changed color on the outside but are still pink and soft in the center. Using a slotted spoon, lift the chicken livers from the pan, transfer them to a large, warmed serving dish or several smaller ones, and keep warm.

Add the sherry to the skillet, increase the heat, and let it bubble for 3–4 minutes to evaporate the alcohol and reduce slightly. At the same time, deglaze the skillet by scraping and stirring all the bits on the bottom of the skillet into the sauce with a wooden spoon. Season the sauce to taste with salt and pepper.

Pour the sherry sauce over the chicken livers and sprinkle over the parsley. Serve piping hot, accompanied by chunks or slices of crusty bread or toast to mop up the sherry sauce.

POTATO WEDGES WITH ROASTED GARLIC DIP

First, make the roasted garlic dip. Preheat the oven to 400°F/200°C. Place the garlic cloves in an ovenproof dish, then pour in the olive oil and toss to coat. Spread out in a single layer and roast in the preheated oven for 25 minutes, or until tender. Remove from the oven and let stand until cool enough to handle.

Peel the garlic cloves, then place on a heavy cutting board and sprinkle with a little salt. Mash well with a fork until smooth. Scrape into a bowl and stir in the sour cream and mayonnaise. Season to taste with salt and paprika. Cover the bowl with plastic wrap and let chill until ready to serve.

To cook the potatoes, cut each potato half into 3 wedges and place in a large bowl. Add the olive oil, garlic, and salt and toss well. Transfer the wedges to a roasting pan, then arrange in a single layer and roast in the preheated oven for 1–1 1/4 hours, or until crisp and golden.

Remove from the oven and transfer to serving bowls. Serve immediately, handing round the roasted garlic dip separately.

SERVES 8
as part of a tapas meal

3 lb/1.3 kg potatoes, unpeeled and halved

2 tbsp Spanish olive oil

1 garlic clove, finely chopped

2 tsp salt

ROASTED GARLIC DIP

2 garlic bulbs, separated into cloves

1 tbsp Spanish olive oil

5 tbsp sour cream or strained plain yogurt

4 tbsp mayonnaise

paprika, to taste

salt

SARDINES WITH ROMESCO SAUCE

SERVES 6
as part of a tapas meal

24 fresh sardines, scaled, cleaned, and heads removed

generous ³/₄ cup all-purpose flour

4 eggs, lightly beaten

9 oz/250 g fresh white bread crumbs

6 tbsp chopped fresh parsley

4 tbsp chopped fresh marjoram

vegetable oil, for deep-frying

ROMESCO SAUCE

1 red bell pepper, halved and seeded

2 tomatoes, halved

4 garlic cloves

¹/₂ cup Spanish olive oil

1 slice white bread, diced

4 tbsp blanched almonds

1 fresh red chile, seeded and chopped

2 shallots, chopped

1 tsp paprika

2 tbsp red wine vinegar

2 tsp sugar

1 tbsp water

First make the sauce. Preheat the oven to 425°F/220°C. Place the bell pepper, tomatoes, and garlic in an ovenproof dish and drizzle over 1 tablespoon of the olive oil, turning to coat. Bake in the preheated oven for 20–25 minutes, then remove from the oven and cool. When cool enough to handle, peel off their skins and place the flesh in a food processor.

Heat 1 tablespoon of the remaining oil in a skillet. Add the bread and almonds and cook over low heat for a few minutes until browned. Remove and drain on paper towels. Add the chile, shallots, and paprika to the pan and cook for 5 minutes, or until the shallots are softened.

Transfer the almond mixture and shallot mixture to the food processor and add the vinegar, sugar, and water. Process to a paste.

With the motor still running, gradually add the remaining oil through the feeder tube. Transfer to a bowl, cover, and reserve.

Place the sardines, skin-side up, on a cutting board and press along the length of the spines with your thumbs. Turn over and remove and discard the bones. Place the flour and eggs in separate bowls. Mix the bread crumbs and herbs together in a third bowl. Toss the fish in the flour, the eggs, then in the bread crumbs.

Heat the vegetable oil in a large pan to 350–375°F/180–190°C, or until a cube of bread browns in 30 seconds. Deep-fry the fish for 4–5 minutes, or until golden and tender. Drain and serve with the sauce.

MOORISH FAVA BEAN DIP

If using fresh fava beans, bring a large pan of lightly salted water to a boil. Add the beans, then reduce the heat and simmer, covered, for 7 minutes. Drain well, then refresh under cold running water and drain again. Remove and discard the outer skins. If using frozen beans, let thaw completely, then remove and discard the outer skins.

Heat 1 tablespoon of the olive oil in a skillet. Add the garlic, onion, and cumin and cook over low heat, stirring occasionally, until the onion is softened and translucent. Add the fava beans and cook, stirring frequently, for 5 minutes.

Remove the skillet from the heat and transfer the mixture to a food processor or blender. Add the lemon juice, the remaining olive oil, water, and mint and process to a paste. Season to taste with salt and pepper.

Scrape the paste back into the skillet and heat gently until warm. Transfer to individual serving bowls and dust lightly with paprika. Serve with dippers of your choice.

**SERVES 6
as part of a tapas
meal**

1 lb 2 oz/500 g shelled
fresh or frozen fava
beans

5 tbsp Spanish olive oil

1 garlic clove, finely
chopped

1 onion, finely chopped

1 tsp ground cumin

1 tbsp lemon juice

3/4 cup water

1 tbsp chopped fresh
mint

salt and pepper

paprika, to garnish

raw vegetables, crusty
bread, or breadsticks,
to serve

index